# FOUR MILES TO FREEDOM

# FOUR MILES TO FREEDOM

## TO FREEDOM

ESCAPE FROM A PAKISTANI POW CAMP

# FAITH JOHNSTON

RANDOM HOUSE INDIA

Published by Random House India in 2013
1

Copyright © Faith Johnston  2013

Random House Publishers India Private Limited
Windsor IT Park, 7th Floor
Tower-B, A-1, Sector 125
Noida 201301, UP

Random House Group Limited
20 Vauxhall Bridge Road
London SW1V 2SA
United Kingdom

978 81 8400 487 8

Typeset in Adobe Garamond by R. Ajith Kumar

Printed and bound in India by Replika Press Private Limited

For sale throughout the world except Canada

*For Manbir*
*and for all those who suffered loss or separation because*
*of the 1971 War*

# Contents

# Contents

# Prologue

Two years ago I sat in Dilip Parulkar's spacious living room in Pune, listening. Dilip was holding a tiny recorder in one hand, leaning forward in a low carved chair. It was late morning and he had just come in from tennis. Still wearing his tennis shorts and jacket, this sturdy man with his square, handsome face and ready smile had now turned his energy to another task. He was starting to tell me the story of how he and two other airmen escaped from a POW camp in Pakistan. I found it strange that he didn't begin at the beginning; instead he dove into the tale very near its end.

'We were sitting on the roadside, over a culvert, wondering whether to hide.' But the matter was not immediately urgent, he said, for though it was broad daylight, there seemed to be no one else for miles around. The landscape on the approach to the Khyber Pass was barren and stony. When they looked down the road they could see the hills that marked the beginning of the pass to Afghanistan (and safety), but for miles around them, the land was almost flat. The only habitations visible were a few walled enclaves in the distance. Dilip wasn't sure if they were small villages or clan compounds.

'So there we were, the three of us, taking a breather, thinking we might soon scoot down the embankment and into the culvert and spend the day hiding there,' he went on. 'Then, in the distance, I saw someone riding across the field on a bicycle. The bicycle was heading straight for us so all we could do was wait as it approached. Obviously it was too late to hide.'

'It was a boy in his teens and a very friendly fellow,' laughs Dilip. 'Curious, too. He wanted to know who we were and where we were from. I tried asking him a few questions, but nothing could divert him for long.'

As a foreigner living in India, I had no trouble imagining this boy and his barrage of questions. India, like Pakistan, is full of gregarious young people who love to question strangers. I meet them every time I step out my door.

The conversation ended when the boy walked onto the road and flagged down a bus, not for himself but for his new friends. He was very concerned. Here were three men returning to their native country after a long absence—men who didn't know the lay of the land at all. 'You can't walk all the way to Landi Kotal,' he told them. 'It is much too far to go on foot.'

Thus three Indian pilots who had planned to hide in a culvert until sunset, ended up making their way up a winding road, then through a long narrow gorge to the summit of the Khyber Pass, in broad daylight on the roof of a bus.

After my introduction to a story that Dilip had told many times over the last forty years, but had never written down, I knew we needed to go back and start again, at the beginning. And I knew the effort would be worth my while. I loved Dilip's humour and his sense of the absurd. This would not be a stuffy, pompous story of battles fought and demons conquered. In fact demons would be in rather short supply in this story. Instead, it would be the tale of a man who had a dream he almost realized, told in a string of vivid, unpredictable moments, like life itself.

**Faith Johnston**
September 2013

## Northwestern India and Pakistan

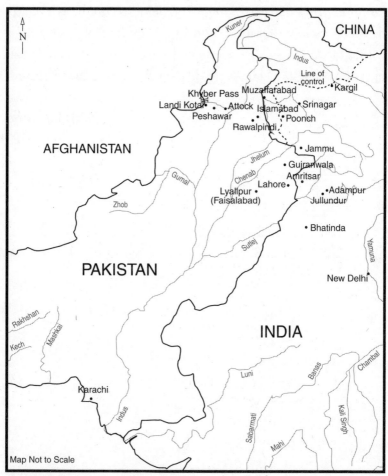

Disclaimer: Other than the official Indian boundaries depicted on the map, some boundaries are as per author's own findings and study. The author and publisher do not claim them to be official or legal boundaries. They are for illustrative purposes.

# Indian Air Force POWs in Pakistan
(December 1971)


Wing Commander B.A. Coelho, 39
Squadron Leader D.S. Jafa, 37 (on 25 December)
Squadron Leader A.V. Kamat, 33
Flight Lieutenant J.L. Bhargava, 29
Flight Lieutenant Tejwant Singh, 29
Flight Lieutenant D.K. Parulkar, 29
Flight Lieutenant M.S. Grewal, 29
Flight Lieutenant Harish Sinhji, 26
Flight Lieutenant A.V. Pethia, 28
Flying Officer V.S. Chati, 25
Flying Officer K.C. Kuruvilla, 26
Flying Officer H.N.D. Mulla-Feroze, 27 (on 5 December)

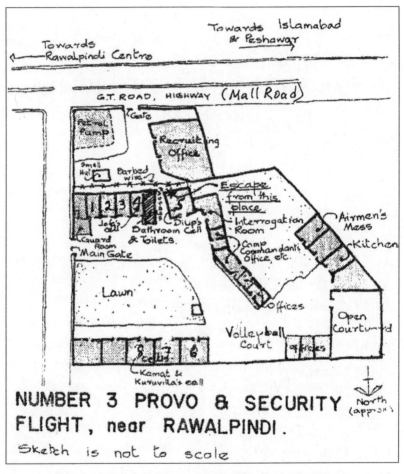

Towards Islamabad & Peshawar

Towards Rawalpindi Centro

G.T. ROAD, HIGHWAY (Mall Road)

Gate

Petrol Pump

Recruiting Office

Small Hut

Barbed wire

1 2 3 4

Jap cell

Dilip's Cell

Bathroom & Toilets.

Escape from this place

Interrogation Room

Camp Commandant's Office, etc.

Airmen's Mess

Kitchen

Guard Room

Main Gate

Offices

Open Courtyard

Lawn

Volleyball Court

offices

8 cells 7 6

Kamat & Kuruvilla's cell

North (approx)

NUMBER 3 PROVO & SECURITY FLIGHT, near RAWALPINDI.

Sketch is not to scale

Harish Sinhji's sketch in P.C. Lal's *My Years With the IAF*, Courtesy of Lancer International, 1986, 2008, p. 353.

# Rawalpindi
## (Midnight, 12 August 1972)

This time the plan worked. The final layer of plaster gave way. The three men crawled out and waited by the wall. When it seemed safe they dashed across the narrow alleyway to the back wall of the next cell block. The storm hadn't broken, but a strong wind fired dust and sand onto their faces. As for the watchman in the adjoining compound, there he was, sitting on his charpoy, perilously close. But when the men took a closer look at him, they realized he had put a blanket over his head!

The prisoners made their way along the back wall of the cell block towards the outer wall. They looked over the wall and down the lane to Mall Road, and were surprised to see a large crowd of people streaming past. Obviously a late show at the cinema had just let out. They decided to wait a few minutes.

As the three men squatted between the rear wall of the cell block and the hut in the recruiting compound, the wind grew fiercer by the moment and it started to rain. In no time the watchman tore the blanket from his head and made a dash for the recruiting centre verandah, carrying both blanket and charpoy. As soon as he had settled there, prone now, with the blanket over his head once more, the prisoners scaled the five-foot wall with no trouble.

By this time the theatre crowd had thinned out. Following Chati's directions, they turned left on Mall Road and kept walking, as if they, too, had come from a late show.

Soon it was pouring, but nothing could dampen their spirits. They were well aware that the stormy weather, first wind, then rain, was the perfect cover for their departure. It was just what they had hoped for.

'Freedom!' exclaimed the ebullient Sinhji as they trudged down Mall Road. His thick black hair was drenched and water was pouring as if from a spout down his boyish face, catching in his long eyelashes.

'Not yet,' replied Grewal with his usual caution. With his height and beard and close cropped head, he hoped to pass for a Pathan. Dilip walked alongside. He too had grown a beard for the occasion and had even had a special suit tailored by a camp attendant. Now the green salwar kurta he'd had made especially for this night was clinging to him like plastic wrap.

But Sinhji was right. For the moment, they were indeed free. It was only a matter of staying free. If everything went well, the alarm would not be raised until morning. That gave them seven or eight hours before anyone started looking for them. And should they be questioned, they had their stories ready. They had decided they would all pose as Christians for they knew little of Islamic prayers and rituals and their ignorance would give them away immediately. Though none of them was actually Christian, each had attended schools with Christians and served in the air force with them, and they knew that Pakistan, too, had a number of Christians in its air force.

As for their names, Dilip and Grewal were LACs Phillip Peters and Ali Ameer, based at PAF station, Lahore. Sinhji was Harold Jacob, an Anglo-Pakistani drummer from Hyderabad in Sind. He had met the other two in Lahore during a recent gig at La Bella Hotel. All this was made up and could easily crumble under questioning. They had no idea if there really was a hotel called La Bella in Lahore, and though Grewal had once had a Christian friend whose name was Ali Ameer, it was hardly a Christian name.

'Remember,' said Dilip, 'no rough stuff.' That had been their pledge from the beginning. They were honourable men, bent on a heroic task. Even if cornered, and a simple crack on the head could get them out of a tight spot, they would not take any violent action. They were going to use their wits, and only their wits.

# Near Jullundur
## (10 December 1971)

That morning Flight Lieutenant Dilip Parulkar took off in formation from Adampur, an Indian Air Force (IAF) base near Jullundur in the Punjab plains of northwestern India. It was the sixth day of the Indo-Pakistan War and Dilip's tenth sortie. This time, instead of providing support for the Indian Army by hitting convoys of Pakistani tanks and transport vehicles, his target was a radar station east of Lahore. The station was proving troublesome and they had been ordered to take it out.

Like all fighter pilots, Dilip had been preparing for war his whole career. In the 1965 War with Pakistan he had been wounded on his first sortie. He had managed to land his Hunter but then had been grounded for the duration. Now he was grateful to have a second chance to use his skills for the honour and defence of his country.

And he had no doubt that the Indian cause was just. Nine

months before, the Pakistani government, led by President Yahya Khan, had refused to step down after the Awami League, based in East Pakistan, won a majority in the national elections. For years the Bengalis in East Pakistan had chaffed under governments that favoured the cultural and economic development of West Pakistan. Now the moderate Awami League, with a clear majority gained in the freest and fairest election in years, could implement its Six Point Plan, giving East Pakistan autonomy in all areas except foreign affairs and defence.

This was not the election result Yahya Khan had expected. With a number of political parties participating, he had hoped for a weak coalition that he and his own supporters could dominate. At first Yahya sought to retain at least some of his power by legitimate means. After the elections he tried to negotiate a power-sharing arrangement with Sheikh Mujibur Rahman, leader of the Awami League, and Zulfikar Ali Bhutto, whose People's Party had gained the majority of votes in West Pakistan, but the negotiations got nowhere. Then, on 1 March 1971, Yahya Khan announced the indefinite postponement of the new National Assembly, which had been slated to meet that month. The people of East Pakistan were outraged. They hit the streets in mass demonstrations and strikes.

As protests in East Pakistan gained momentum, Yahya Khan recanted and proposed that the National Assembly meet on 25 March. In light of later events it appears that this announcement was not made in good faith. Instead, it was a stalling tactic so that he could prepare for a military crackdown. On 25 March Yahya curtailed negotiations and both he and Bhutto flew home from Dacca that day. Later that evening the Pakistan Army went on a killing spree that targeted supporters of the Awami League, students at Dacca University, leading intellectuals, Bengali members of the military and police forces, and others who got in their way. Foreign journalists were confined to their quarters and flown out of the country the next day. In the midst of the mayhem, Sheikh Mujibur Rahman was arrested and charged with treason.

There was nothing provoked or spontaneous about the army's response that night and in the days and nights that followed. Clearly, they were following orders. Altogether it is estimated that the Pakistan Army killed 2,00,000 people in East Pakistan, and others died as they fled across the border into India.

All pleas for the international community to intervene failed because Pakistan had the support of the United States. The Cold War led to some glaring injustices, and the plight of East Pakistan (now Bangladesh) was certainly one of them. At the time of the massacre in East Pakistan, Richard Nixon was well into his first term as president of the United States. His main foreign policy goal was to achieve détente with China (and ultimately the Soviet Union) in order to extricate his country from the war in Vietnam.

Since the United States had no diplomatic relations with the People's Republic of China, Nixon and his White House security advisor, Henry Kissinger, initially relied on Pakistan's president, Yahya Khan, to facilitate arrangements with China. The first step in these negotiations was a secret meeting between Chinese Foreign Minister Zhou Enlai and Kissinger. Kissinger flew from Karachi to Beijing in July 1971. Until that meeting took place, and even after it, Nixon and Kissinger, though fully informed of events in East Pakistan, refused to ruffle Yahya Khan's feathers by counselling restraint or cutting aid.

Meanwhile India bore the brunt of supporting a rapidly increasing number of refugees. By mid-July over six million refugees had fled East Pakistan and more were arriving every day. By November, just before war broke out, there were almost ten million. The Indian government decided, in secret, that unless Pakistan could devise a viable political settlement to get the refugees back home, India would have to gradually move to war.

The Awami League declared the independence of Bangladesh on 26 March and formed a guerilla army of freedom fighters called the Mukti Bahini. India supported the Mukti Bahini, again in secret, but it postponed recognizing the independence of Bangladesh. To do so would provoke Pakistan to war immediately, and India needed time to prepare. Indira Gandhi's army chief hoped for a delay until at least November. By then the monsoon would be over and the tidal rivers of East Pakistan easier to bridge. And just in case China decided to join the fray, the Himalayan passes along the Indian–Chinese border would be clogged with snow.

While planning for war, but hoping by some miracle for peace, Indira Gandhi and her emissaries made the rounds of world capitals more than once, pleading for action against Pakistan and help for the refugees. In August India signed a friendship treaty with the Soviet Union which did not mention defence but was intended to deter the Chinese from joining a war against India. Gandhi's last stop on her final round in early November was Washington, but by that time it was too late for any American pressure on Yahya to succeed. Pakistan, too, was preparing for war. It was just a matter of how and when.

Since late in March the Indian Air Force had been on standby, ready to move to the front at two hours' notice. Forward units had some of their aircraft armed and ready for action at all times. Still, training continued, and Dilip Parulkar spent those tense months training pilots on the Kiran jet trainer at Dundigal, an IAF flying school north of Hyderabad. In November he was ordered to join his squadron, the 26th. Along with two other pilots he flew out the next day. 'We definitely knew it meant war,' he remembers, and he was not happy at the thought of fighting on the western front.

'Having trained as a fighter pilot, I was itching to fight. I wanted to put my training to use. But in this case I felt that going pell-mell into operations against West Pakistan was not a good idea. We were going to lose lives, equipment and aircraft, when really the central aim of the war was to advance on the eastern front. I remember standing in a bar in Adampur and holding forth on the subject that we should do nothing in the western sector that would cause us losses.'

Otherwise he was not sorry to be in Adampur, which was a major, heavily defended forward base with facilities for three squadrons. By the time he arrived, all the fighters were sheltered in blast pens and the army had set up perimeter patrols and anti-aircraft artillery. But Dilip's time there was short, even shorter than he expected. His task was to get up to speed once again on the Sukhoi 7, the IAF's newest and largest supersonic fighter. And he hoped also to see his good friend, Major Inder Khanna, who was stationed with a battalion in nearby Amritsar. In fact Dilip had just returned from seeing Inder the night of 3

December when the Pakistani Air Force (PAF) made a number
of pre-emptive strikes on the western front. He remembers
the attacks being 'absolutely ineffective—just a show of force.
They were saving their air force for future attacks.' And so the
war began.

From 4 December the 26th Squadron was flying sorties every
day, some days more than one. By 10 December losses were
already heavy. Out of eighteen pilots, two had been downed
by ground fire. By the end of the twelve-day war, the toll for
the 26th Squadron alone would stand at three pilots dead and
two captured.

As Dilip flew from Adampur the morning of 10 December,
none of these matters weighed heavily. It was his tenth mission,
the tenth time he had been briefed about the weather, followed
by a briefing on the forward line of India's troops (FLOT). It was
the tenth time he had stuffed 200 Pakistani rupees in his pocket
and strapped a loaded .38 revolver to his leg, in case he had to
eject and were beset by an angry mob. But he wasn't nervous.
He remembers feeling relaxed. 'Nothing's going to happen to
me,' he thought. He always had an air of invincibility, a devil-
may-care attitude that his colleagues remember.

His reputation for luck had been reinforced during the
Indo-Pakistan War of 1965. Although fully operational on the
Hunter only a week before that war started, Dilip had been
in Delhi when his squadron commander answered a call for
replacements from another squadron that had experienced heavy
losses. Dilip and another pilot grabbed their helmets and took
off immediately. Forty minutes later they reached Halwara, a
base near the front.

Although Dilip was hit in his first sortie from Halwara, through a combination of good luck and competent flying, he had managed to save both his plane and his life. The target that day was a column of tanks. When they reached the target, the Hunters were greeted by ack-ack from anti-aircraft guns mounted on the tanks. Dilip, flying fourth, got the worst of it. The first plane can count on the element of surprise, but by the time the fourth makes its attack the gunners have had the time to correct and coordinate their fire.

Just into the dive, Dilip's Hunter was hit. Suddenly the cockpit filled with mist and ambient noise as cooler air and the sound of guns penetrated the cockpit. A half-inch bullet had pierced the floor of the cockpit and hit his right shoulder before exiting through the Plexiglas canopy.

He was lucky. If he hadn't been leaning forward to peer through the gun sight his head would have been in the path of the bullet.

As Dilip pulled out of the attack he felt a sharp pain in his arm and realized his G-suit was already soaked with blood. He decided not to report it. He was afraid the attack might be aborted if he mentioned he had been wounded. Once the four planes had exited the target area, he radioed that he had been hit in the right arm and was bleeding profusely. His flight commander suggested he eject as soon as they reached Indian territory. 'You might be able to fly with one arm,' he said, 'but you'll never be able to land.'

But Dilip hadn't heeded that advice. He'd been determined to try a landing. He was successful on his second attempt.

An inspection of Parulkar's Hunter revealed that he had made the right decision. After piercing his shoulder the bullet had gone through the headrest and the top of the ejection seat. In the process, it had severely frayed the static line that connects the drogue parachute with the main parachute. Had he ejected, the main chute would not have deployed.

Now, six years later, Dilip was flying his single-engine Russian fighter one hundred metres above the Punjab plains. He was travelling at a speed of a thousand kilometres an hour. Below him the wheat and cane were a blur of green. There was no time to think of luck or fate or invincibility. That was what he loved about flying. When you fly fighters there is no time to think of anything but the present task. It requires all your concentration.

# Capture

Their target that morning was only 125 kilometres from Adampur and they reached it in less than ten minutes, flying low all the way. One by one the SU7s rose and dove, firing their rockets and dropping bombs. As usual Dilip was in fourth position. He remembers seeing his colleagues hit the target.

That was his last clear memory for several days. The memories he does have are brief, like photo flashes with nothing to connect them.

He vaguely remembers the plane being hit and going out of control. 'I was lucky the plane pitched upwards, not downwards. I remember ejecting. It was almost a reflex. There was no choice. It was very different in 1965—I had a choice then.'

'Ejecting is like shooting a bullet,' he explains, 'and you are the bullet.'

His next memory is of a mob of people surrounding him and beating him with sticks, fists, feet. When he tells this story, his listeners often respond with, 'Oh, how terrible!' but Dilip has never seen it that way. 'We were attacking these people. Their homes were being destroyed. I didn't expect them to run up and kiss me!'

He remembers riding in the back of a truck, blindfolded. It is a long ride and very cold. His head and knees are bandaged but it isn't his bruises and scrapes that are bothering him. One of his feet is freezing. He realizes he is missing his boot and that his foot is completely bare. 'Where is my boot?' he keeps asking.

Then he is in a cold, damp, dimly lit cell, God knows where. The cell is about seven feet by eight and has no window. The only furniture is a charpoy. The single light bulb in the ceiling, controlled by a switch outside, is never turned off. For days he wears the shirt and pants he had put on the morning of 10 December. The mob had ripped off his G-suit and taken everything else, including the revolver, the Pakistani currency and his watch. But the G-suit, or flying overall, is what he misses most because of the cold. He has two blankets. He puts one under him and one over but it's still impossible to warm up, even in the middle of the day. Meals are delivered to the cell and when he needs the toilet he reaches through the bars of an inner door to an outer door made of wood and knocks. A guard comes eventually with handcuffs and a blindfold and leads him to the toilet.

Several times he is handcuffed and blindfolded and taken to a larger room for interrogation. He actually looks forward to interrogation because it is very cold and the interrogator always begins with the question, 'Would you like a cup of tea?' and then sends for two cups of tea, one for himself, and one for Dilip.

And it is much better tea than that delivered to the cells twice a day. Sometimes there is even a second cup.

The interrogators threaten death, but they never touch him. He finds the whole thing ridiculous. It is the typical good cop, bad cop routine. When you get the good cop he tries to be chummy. 'What did you do in Delhi for fun?' the good cop asks him once.

The bad cop is equally predictable. He threatens Dilip, calls him an infidel dog, and curses India. It is all so clearly an act that Dilip doesn't take it seriously. 'But I didn't take anything very seriously then,' he remembers. 'Everything was a lark.'

After several days he still has no idea where he is. The interrogators seek information—mainly technical questions about the Sukhoi 7 and airfield defence—but they are willing to give no information themselves, and the guards are the same.

Then one day he has a stroke of luck. The hole in the wooden door is covered by a cardboard flap on the outside. Whenever the guards want to observe the prisoner, day or night, they lift the flap and look in. Dilip discovers that if he reaches through the bars and pushes the flap out just a little he can see the path in front of his cell. He already knows from his trips back and forth to the toilet that his cell faces a courtyard, with the toilet located on the other side. One day he pushes out the flap at just the right moment to glimpse a guard's trousers and belt buckle; on the buckle is engraved 'Rawalpindi Police'.

The interrogations continue. One day, the bad cop asks him to draw a map of the Adampur airfield. He can picture the airfield clearly, both from the air and from the ground—all the rows of blast pens sheltering the fighters, the anti-aircraft guns, the troops patrolling the perimeter. But he decides to give them a sketch map of the Santa Cruz airport in Bombay instead. All pilots in India knew that airport well.

'"Where are the guns?" asks the bad cop. "Where are the anti-aircraft missiles?" So I drew them at random.'

'The man left the room with the sketch and came back livid. "You've been fooling with us," he said. "Do you want to go home alive or not?" He knew I didn't take him seriously. He was so furious that he had me face the corner and didn't let me sit down. He told the guard in Urdu, "If he tries anything, shoot him."' Dilip got the message.

'Not being fed didn't bother me but I did get tired of standing. Once I started to squat, but then I heard the guard loading his rifle so I changed my mind and stood up again. A little later the guard said, "Sahib, your legs must be paining. You sit down. If someone comes, I will cough and you stand up."'

The kindness of that guard warms his heart even forty years later. And so does the full story of his rescue, which he learned about later. One day a civilian policeman appeared at the camp, dressed in uniform, and asked to see him. He was a chap of about forty, with a twinkle in his eye, obviously very pleased with himself. He told Dilip that he had been on duty the day Dilip's plane was downed and he had been surrounded by an angry mob. 'I called a halt to the beating,' the policeman said. 'I told them "this guy is worth more to us alive than dead," and they stopped.' The policeman had taken Dilip to the airbase where he was given first aid. But his interest hadn't stopped there. He had travelled all the way from Lahore to Pindi to find out how he was faring.

15

One day an American interrogates Dilip. A tall man of about fifty, with blue eyes, he is wearing the one-star insignia of a brigadier general in the US Air Force. He sports an impressive row of medals, and is both friendly and physically imposing, as Americans tend to be. When he introduces himself he is disappointed that Dilip does not recognize his name immediately. The man's main interest is gathering technical information about the Sukhoi 7.

Later, when the downed pilots meet and compare notes, they are surprised and impressed but also outraged to learn that they had been interrogated by Chuck Yeager—an important guy, no doubt about that. In 1947 he had been the first pilot to break the sound barrier and later, in the 1960s, he'd trained astronauts for the American space programme. But what was he doing in Pakistan?

Dilip and his mates all agree that the Pakistani Air Force has the right to question them. And they have the right to give only name, rank and serial number, and any innocuous information they can cough up in order save their necks. But what right has this American? They plan, when they get back home, to report this incident. 'How about sending a mission to North Vietnam?' they will say. 'I think we need to interrogate some downed American pilots there.'

Later still, they learn that right at the end of his career (1971–73), Chuck Yeager served as an advisor to the Pakistan Air Force. During the 1971 War, Yeager's own twin-engine Beechcraft had been destroyed in an Indian Air Force raid on the Chaklala air base near Rawalpindi. They will also learn that in the hope of pressuring the American government to supply

Pakistan with more planes, Yeager had predicted India could win a war against Pakistan in two weeks. He had certainly been right about that.

On 16 December, six days after Dilip's capture, Pakistan's army in the east surrenders, and the following day the war is over. India has won an amazing victory, due largely to careful preparation, air superiority, and the swift advance of the Indian Army into Bangladesh. At the outset of the war the Pakistani Air Force had only one squadron in the east, stationed in Dacca. On 6 December, only two days into the war, IAF Mig-21s bombed the Dacca airfield with such force and accuracy that the lone PAF squadron there was grounded for the duration. From that day on Pakistani ground troops had no protection from the air, so Indian paratroopers and helicopters could leap ahead of their own ground forces with little opposition.

As a result of India's support Bangladesh now has its independence. Pakistan holds approximately 600 POWs, including twelve airmen, while India and Bangladesh hold a whopping 93,000 POWs.

The news of the extent of the victory takes weeks to reach the IAF POWs in Pakistan. They are pretty sure the war has ended; they no longer hear the whine of air raid sirens, the rumble of heavy planes taking off or landing at the air base nearby. But who has won? Are they winners or losers? Dilip would like to know. He would like to chat up the guards on his trips back and forth to the toilet, but they seem to be a surly lot. Either they are obeying orders, or actively hostile, he isn't sure which.

If the war is really over he knows that the next step will be a prisoner exchange. After the 1965 War, Pakistan held seven

IAF pilots prisoner for four months. From what he's heard, they had a rough experience, though the medical care was all right. One of those prisoners was the son of the Army Chief of Staff, General Cariappa. He was offered preferential treatment but refused it, and so did his father, on his behalf. He's also heard that the PAF POWs held in India were treated very well. The IAF had considerable sympathy for the PAF pilots whose chances of survival were poor because their Sabres lacked good low-level ejection seats. In Delhi the three surviving pilots were lodged in a posh area, not far from the prime minister's residence, and they were guarded by IAF officers. According to rumour, they were even taken to Connaught Place for a movie.

Dilip wonders what kind of treatment he can expect now that the war has ended, and how long it will take to negotiate a prisoner exchange this time. But that isn't his main concern. He knew several of the pilots captured in 1965. When they returned to India, his first question to them was, 'Did you try to escape?' and their answer was 'no'.

The question of capture is something all fighter pilots have to take seriously. Ending up a POW is an occupational hazard. If your plane goes down, it usually happens in enemy territory. After 1965 Dilip had decided that if he were captured, he would make every effort to escape. His vow was not a secret. In 1969, over dinner in Delhi with his commanding officer Wing Commander M.S. Bawa and his wife, he mentioned his intention.

'No,' said Bawa, 'it would be far too dangerous. Don't be a fool.'

'It would be my duty,' Dilip told Bawa. 'Isn't it the duty of every POW to escape if at all possible?'

But for Dilip escape wasn't just a matter of duty. Planning and executing an escape, using his wits to counter all obstacles, this was the ultimate adventure. He'd watched Steve McQueen in *The Great Escape*. Of course the story was jazzed up for the movies but most of it was true; over seventy airmen had tunnelled their way out of a German POW camp during World War II. They had mustered all their determination and ingenuity to design and dig a series of tunnels. They had forged documents and scrounged clothing that would pass as civvies. Then they had taken their chances.

And he'd read *Papillon,* too, the story of Henri Charrière's escape from Devil's Island in French Guyana. How clever Charrière had been, watching the waves, observing that every seventh wave was the most powerful, that flotsam thrown on that wave never came back. He'd made himself a raft of coconuts and floated out to sea. For Dilip, it was a lesson in confidence and determination and, above all, in perseverance. And now his turn had come. Why not an Indian escape story for a change?

It isn't long after the 1971 War ends that little by little the routine at the prison in Rawalpindi begins to ease. Occasionally the wooden door on Dilip's cell is left open, and one day he sees another prisoner being led, blindfolded, to the toilet. He's a very tall, slim fellow. Even without seeing his face Dilip thinks he recognizes the man. 'Vikram!' he calls out. 'Is that you?' Dilip and Flight Lieutenant Aditya Vikram Pethia had been flying instructors together.

The next time he sees Pethia being led past, he begins to joke with him and another voice joins in, from the cell on his left. 'Is that you, Dilip?' the voice says. 'I'm Kamy.' He had met Squadron Leader Kamat only once in the Adampur mess, just before the war. Kamy had ejected late and his parachute had not fully opened by the time he hit the ground. He had suffered multiple fractures in both legs and was in plaster from his ankles to his groin.

Soon after this, interrogations end and the guards dispense with the handcuffs and blindfolds on the trips to the toilet. Dilip can see that the camp is a walled compound with several clusters of cells and offices set around an open yard. In typical military fashion there is a guardhouse at the gate. In the same block as the guardhouse are four solitary cells. The place wasn't built to house more than four prisoners at a time. All the other cells, including Dilip's, have been improvised from offices or storage rooms.

After taking stock of the lay of the land, Dilip devises his first plan of escape. He observes that at any one time there are four or five armed guards on patrol. One of them, the one in charge, is always a PAF corporal. At night the corporal sits in the guardhouse, making rounds occasionally. The others, posted around the compound, are young jawans from the army. They work in shifts around the clock, and those on the night shift are inevitably weary.

His plan is to ask to be taken to the toilet in the middle of the night. On the way there or back he will grab the guard's gun from his holster and take him hostage. Then he will demand a plane for Delhi. It isn't an original idea—he's heard of an Italian fellow using a hostage to hijack a plane in the USA and divert it to Italy. It is a plan that just might work. And it is the only one he can think of at the moment.

# Rawalpindi
## (13 August 1972)

After they had walked about a hundred yards down Mall Road, all the street lights went out. They kept walking happily along despite the dark and the rain and, following Chati's instructions, turned left onto another broad road. After walking for close to an hour along deserted streets, they came to a junction that was hopping with life despite the hour and the power failure. Here, at last, was the interstate bus station and right beside them was a bus with its engine idling.

'Peshawar, jana hai bhai?' shouted the driver. 'Peshawar, Peshawar!' The three men hopped on immediately and took seats towards the back of the bus, near the rear exit.

'We climbed in hoping the bus would start off quickly,' remembers Sinhji. 'However, it held on till it was packed to capacity and that took about an hour. What was uncomfortable is that the conductor asked us in broken English for the fare.

Normally it is only Urdu, not pure Urdu but something similar
to our Hindustani that is spoken all over. Even PAF officers greet
each other with 'salaam alekum', not good morning. So this
attempt at English by the smiling conductor made us rather self-
conscious but all we could do was sit tight and hope for the best.'

They slouched in their seats, heads down, pretending to doze
and eventually, at around 2.30 a.m., the bus set off. They were
all puzzled by their lack of success in passing themselves off as
locals. What was it that gave them away?  Not their speech,
for they'd hardly said a word. It must be something in their
appearance. But none of them, even forty years later, is sure
what it was. Grewal still wore his Sikh kada, his steel bracelet,
for it wouldn't come off, but he'd made sure it was tucked up
under the sleeve of his shirt. Granted, a long-sleeved dress shirt
is not the same as a kurta and looks rather odd worn with a
traditional salwar. But the problem may have been the clothes
they had saved for the escape—the dress shirts worn by Sinjhi
and Grewal, even Dilip's salwar-kurta were so obviously new,
so little worn, that everyone else on the bus looked shabby by
comparison. Or maybe it was their canvas shoes. Everyone else
was wearing chappals.

At Attock, halfway to Peshawar, there was a halt. Everyone
piled out and sat on benches at a dhaba, drinking cups of milky
tea. Apart from the feeble light from the dhaba, the night was
still pitch dark. Nearby was the mighty Indus River, which had
figured so largely in the debate about escape routes, but they
could neither see nor hear it. They could have been anywhere.
They could have been at home, stopping at Karnal or Ambala
en route to Delhi.

# Christmas Day
## (1971)

At five o'clock on 25 December, all the POWs in the Pindi camp assembled for a special tea. They were taken, one by one, to a room that would accommodate all of them. By this time most of them had guessed that the camp was a small one for Indian Air Force prisoners only. Some of the able-bodied, who had been captured earlier than Dilip, had already been taken outside to a courtyard where they could warm up in the sun and get some exercise. But on Christmas, all twelve, even the injured, were brought together for a party.

Dilip found that he knew half of them. Two were his batchmates. He had trained at the flying academy in Jodhpur and again in Secunderabad with Flight Lieutenants Tejwant Singh and Jawahar Lal Bhargava. There was Singh, the only obvious Sikh in the group, with his dark beard and neatly tied white turban. And there was Bhargava, known as Brother Bhargava by all his mates—his high forehead was thrust back as he listened to one man after another and called each one 'brother'.

But it had been a long time since his training days, and Dilip had been posted with some of the others, too. Wing Commander Coelho, the most senior officer among the prisoners, had been flight commander of a Hunter squadron Dilip had served in. Coelho, who would be close to forty now, looked somewhat sombre but held himself together, making the rounds and going through the necessary courtesies as senior officer. His hair was beginning to grey, just a little, over the ears.

At the beginning of the war Coelho had been commanding a squadron on the eastern front. After the IAF quickly gained control of the air there, Coelho and his squadron had been transferred to the western front where fighting was still heavy. He had been shot down on 9 December, the day before Dilip.

Squadron Leader Jafa, who was second in seniority, was from Dilip's own squadron, the 26th. He had been serving as Aide de Camp (ADC) to Air Chief P.C. Lal before the war, but had opted to return to active service with his squadron in Adampur. He was shot down on 5 December, the second day of the war. His mates believed he had ejected safely and they were right. Here he was, suffering pain from a spinal injury, but otherwise his urbane, confident self.

Flight Lieutenant Aditya Vikram Pethia, whom Dilip had encountered already, looked particularly pale and fragile despite his height, and Squadron Leader Kamat, a heavyset fellow, was weighed down further by the casts on his legs.

Dilip knew another Sikh in the group, Flight Lieutenant M.S. Grewal, who wore his hair short and his beard trimmed.

With his grey eyes and brown hair, Grewal could easily pass as a European, or a Pathan for that matter. Dilip and Grewal had been posted at the same station once and had played hockey and squash together.

The other four pilots, the ones Dilip didn't know, were several years younger than he was. Apart from Flying Officer Kuruvilla, a tall, fit-looking fellow, none of them was in good shape. Flying Officer Chati, the youngest of the POWs, was long and lanky, too thin really, and one side of his face was bandaged. He said very little and when the cake was cut the poor man ate it with difficulty. Flight Lieutenant Harish Sinjhi was a slightly built young man with a thick head of hair, long eyelashes, and broad lips. Good-looking in a boyish way, if it weren't for the scrapes and bruises. Flying Officer Mulla-Feroze, a little older than the other junior men, and certainly the most pugnacious despite his small frame, had one arm bandaged and in a sling. It was a blessing that without mirrors none of the men had any idea of his own appearance. Dilip's unshaven face was scratched and bruised. He was wearing canvas shoes without laces, as were some of the others. Only a few had managed to keep their flying boots.

Soon the camp commandant arrived with a Christian padre. The commandant's name was Squadron Leader Usman Hamid. He was a good-looking man of medium height and a very gentle manner. The prisoners had already met him individually, and they liked him from the start. Now in excellent English he wished them all a merry Christmas and introduced the padre. After the padre said a prayer, Usman asked Coelho, as senior officer, to cut the cake. Coelho was one of two Christians in the group; Kuruvilla was the other. But many of the POWs had attended Christian schools, so celebrating Christmas was not a novelty. They could have sung *Silent Night* or *Come All Ye Faithful* if asked.

They appreciated Usman Hamid's gesture of bringing them together on Christmas, though no one was in a mood to celebrate, not just yet. Most of them were still in pain from hard landings and beatings by angry villagers. But their state of health was not the only reason they were not in a party mood. Unfortunately, Hamid had chosen to set up the party in the room previously used for interrogations.

'As soon as the camp commandant and the padre left, we checked out the place, looking for microphones. We checked the fans, felt under all the chairs and tables,' remembers Dilip. Grewal remembers finding 'No.3 Provost and Security Flight' stamped on the backs of the chairs, but in terms of hidden microphones, they found nothing. Still they were not ready to confide in one another. Even if the walls didn't have ears, who knew if someone among them might have collaborated, and might continue to pass along information? It was hard to break the ice, especially on that first day.

But it was a great relief to have Tejwant Singh confirm that India had won the war. He had been shot down on his 24th mission on 17 December, just before the ceasefire was declared. (Singh was the only pilot shot down in an air fight. The others had all been downed by ground fire.) On 16 December, from Amritsar, he had watched the surrender of Pakistan's eastern army on TV. Now they all knew that Bangladesh had gained its independence, with their help. The news they'd hoped and prayed for was finally confirmed. It was all that mattered for the moment. Dilip returned to his cell in a buoyant mood. 'Our morale was touching the skies,' he remembers.

The morale in India mirrored that in the Pindi camp. There was great pride everywhere, in India's victory, and more good news was to follow. On 20 December  Yahya Khan resigned in favour of Zulfikar Ali Bhutto. Though Bhutto was no lover of India (he was known in India as Pakistan's foreign minister during the Indo-Pakistan War of 1965), his was the first civilian administration in Pakistan since 1958. In early January Bhutto announced that he was ready for peace talks with India and said that he would release unconditionally Sheikh Mujibur Rahman  from his nine month sojourn in prison. True to his word, Bhutto released Rahman on 8 January and two days later Rahman returned to Dacca in triumph to take up his post as provisional president of Bangladesh.

Even more important for India was the return and resettlement of Bangla refugees. According to the *Times of India*, by 6 January more than 4,00,000 refugees had returned home and an average of 64,000 were returning daily.

All this good news was of little comfort to the families of POWs who didn't yet know if their loved ones were alive or dead. While Dilip Parulkar rejoiced in the Indian victory, his parents back in Nagpur were unsure whether to mourn his death or to keep their hopes alive. No one on the mission had seen him eject. When he didn't return to Adampur on 10 December, he was classified as missing. It was sobering news. All his comrades believed he was dead. And if Dilip—with all his luck—had gone down, what chance did the rest of them have?

For his parents, the waiting, the not knowing, was

excruciatingly painful. They had already lived on pins and needles for years because of their son's passion for flying. It had all started on 15 August 1947, as India celebrated its newly won independence. There was an air show in Nagpur that day, and five-year-old Dilip was taken to the Nagpur airport on his father's bicycle. There they watched as a Tiger Moth performed aerobatics. 'I was so thrilled,' Dilip remembers, 'that on the way home I told my father "I'm going to be a fighter pilot."'

That idea did not sit well with his parents. There was no military tradition his family. His father was an English teacher. And everyone knew that being a fighter pilot was a risky business. No way would the Parulkars consider allowing their only son to take up such a dangerous career. They consulted astrologists, palmists and fortune tellers, all of whom gave the same answer, the only one his parents wanted to hear. 'No, he will not become a pilot,' one astrologist told them. 'He may be a doctor, or perhaps an oilman.' Dilip's parents breathed a sigh of relief.

In 1953, when Dilip was eleven years old, a second son was born. One of his aunts remembers him looking at the new baby, then turning to his mother and saying, 'Now I'm going to be a fighter pilot.' From that point on he had his parents' reluctant permission. His goal was to enter the National Defence Academy (NDA), an institution that provides initial education and training for officers in all three services. 'I was an average plus student most of the time, and liked to play the fool, but I did get coaching for exams.' At the age of fifteen he managed to pass the entrance exams and series of interviews.

He would be at the NDA, near Pune, for the next three years. The first two years involved common education and training for all the cadets, regardless of service. In the final year, half the training was service-specific. For the air cadets this meant practise in winch-launched gliding. But the training was only part of the attraction. Three years at the NDA built a strong sense of brotherhood, of camaraderie for all who attended. They would carry this into every phase of their careers. It was at the NDA that Dilip met Inder Khanna who was to become one of his closest friends.

From the NDA, those cadets destined for the air force moved on to the flying academy at Jodhpur where they trained first on a Hindustan Trainer 2 and then on a Harvard/Texan. Then, for the fighter pilots, it was on to Secunderabad for jet training on the Vampire. Dilip was training in Secunderabad in October 1962, when the Chinese mounted a surprise attack on India's northern border with Tibet. The Sino-Indian War ended in a negotiated settlement a month later, but for the armed forces there was continuing fallout. Suddenly the western world saw India as an ally against Communist China. Previously India had had to pay for all its planes, equipment, and training, but now there were offers of support.

For Dilip and other pilots-in-training, the first opportunity was helicopter training in Britain or France. Anyone who agreed to switch from fighter training to helicopter training would leave for Europe within two weeks, and on return would receive his commission three months early.

'In those days,' says Dilip, 'going to Europe was impossible unless you were very wealthy. Everyone wanted to go. My cousin, Uday Barve, who had gone through the NDA with me and was with me training on the Vampires, said, "Dilip, let's go!" but I was not tempted. I wanted to be a fighter pilot and that was that!'

Because of the urgency of expanding India's armed forces, jet training that year was compressed. Commissioning for pilot officers in the fighter stream was set for 9 March 1963. On 3 March, Dilip watched his cousin Uday take off on a routine training flight. The Vampire's engine failed immediately after takeoff. There was no ejection seat so no possibility of ejection. Uday attempted a forced landing but hit three electrical poles. The plane caught fire and crashed a few kilometres from the airport.

Dilip was in shock. He and Uday had been constant companions since childhood. They were closer than many brothers. Dilip's parents pressured him to quit. 'My father rushed to Hyderabad and offered to pay the entire cost of my training to get me out of the air force, but I held fast and gradually they accepted it.'

The commissioning took place as scheduled, but Dilip did not celebrate as he might have with a few drinks. For a boy from a pious Hindu family, drinking was not acceptable. Of course, he had tried it anyway, and many a night Uday had helped him back to the barracks after a few too many. Every time that happened Uday had pleaded with Dilip to stop drinking.

Immediately after the commissioning ceremonies, Dilip skipped off. He was AWOL for over a week. He spent several days at home, resisting his father's pleas to give up the IAF. Then he decided, as a tribute to Uday, that he would never drink again. It was a vow that served him well in prison. Wanting a drink, needing a drink, would have added another aggravation.

After his commissioning, Dilip was posted to Jorhat in Assam. Weeks after Uday's death he confessed in a letter to Inder Khanna that there were still days when he suddenly missed his cousin, but most of the time he was back to being his 'jolly old self'. He and his mates lived in bamboo huts that were comfortable enough, and because it was an ops area discipline was somewhat relaxed. When they'd finished flying for the day, they would take off on their motorcycles in a gang of seven or eight for neighbouring towns. There they had the use of two posh clubs built by tea planters. Each club had a big wooden dancing floor, a picture hall, tennis courts, and a swimming pool and one even had polo grounds and a golf course.

In the fall of 1963 Dilip, by another stroke of luck, was sent to the UK for training on the Hunter. But he found his first trip overseas not much fun after all. While he loved the flying, he found the weather bitterly cold, and since the IAF gave them only enough money for necessities, dating was out of the question. The only compensation after a long day's work was watching sports on television. Apart from the flying, it was a rather dreary life for a twenty-one-year-old.

# Settling In

Soon after the Christmas party, living conditions at the camp began to improve. Each prisoner was issued a long-sleeved shirt and pants in cotton serge and an olive green sweater (the basic winter uniform for enlisted men in the Pakistani Air Force). They were still cold, but the new clothes were an improvement on the ragtag wardrobe they'd been wearing, even though most of them were a poor fit. Now that interrogations were over, it seemed that Master Warrant Officer (MWO) Rizvi, the second in command, was doing all that was within his power to make them comfortable. He gave all the men toothbrushes and towels, but no razors. And it was Rizvi, early on, who had supplied Tejwant Singh with his white turban.

One day Rizvi told Coelho that he had served in the Royal Indian Air Force before Partition. His family came from Kanpur. 'I've heard the name Coelho before,' Rizvi said. 'My father was in the British army and he often mentioned a Brigadier Coelho.'

'Brigadier Coelho was my father,' Coelho told him.

And so a link was established between Coelho and Rizvi. 'The first month was hell,' Coelho remembers, 'but after that things settled down.'

Many muhajirs (1947 refugees) from India, like Rizvi, had settled in the Punjab of which Rawalpindi was the capital, and the prisoners encountered them more than once. When Kuruvilla was taken to the hospital for an X-ray, he met a Tamilian who was very happy to have the chance to speak his own language again. A lascar at the camp, who had migrated from Patiala, was eager to question Bhargava, who knew Patiala well because he had studied there. It was surprising that despite the trauma of their 1947 displacement, the muhajirs were always friendly. Twenty-five years is not a long time in the scheme of things. Memories of India were still strong and not all of them were bad memories.

Among the prisoners, both Grewal and Tejwant Singh had fled Pakistan with their families in 1947, but since they were only four and five years old at the time, they had few memories to draw on. What they did possess was fluency in Punjabi, which proved an advantage in dealing with most of the camp staff.

But even more vital to the POWs recovery than the improved relations with the staff was the end of solitary confinement, which had been as stressful as the interrogations. The prisoners had all found those first weeks after capture disorienting, lonely and frightening, and most of their fears were entirely reasonable. Who knew they had survived and were prisoners of war? Only their Pakistani captors, which meant they were completely at their mercy.

'My worst time,' says Tejwant Singh, 'was the initial days

after capture when days went by and nights came and the interrogators came and went and I didn't know what was in store. Before we all met on 25 December one person came to my cell and threatened me with dire consequences because I had given incorrect names of the pilots in my squadron. He said I was trying to be very smart and that they had not yet declared my name. So when we met on the 25th I was very relieved that someone had seen me alive.'

Kuruvilla was held in solitary confinement for several days before being interrogated. He encountered no one but a silent guard who delivered food and put a hood over his head for his trips to the toilet. Finally he was at the end of his tether and could stand it no longer. He pounded on the door until the guard came.

'I can't be treated like this,' he told him. 'It's against the Geneva Convention.' He asked for a piece of paper so that he could record his complaint. The next thing he knew a heavyset man in his fifties or sixties appeared at his door with a paper and pencil. It was Rizvi to the rescue. It seemed like a miracle. Kuru had what he needed. He had suddenly gone from being no one to being a person who merited the attention of this affable little man.

One day, when Bhargava was still in solitary confinement, Rizvi suggested he might like to have a shave. A barber soon arrived with a very rough razor—not a pleasant experience. Then a strange thing happened, something that had nothing to do with the rough shave; Bhargava began to weep. The tears ran down his face and they wouldn't stop. The barber was alarmed and went off to report the matter.

Before long Usman Hamid paid a visit. 'I think you are lonely,' he said. 'I'm going to move you in with someone else for a few days.'

After Christmas, the painful experience of solitary confinement ended and all the prisoners were allowed to meet each day. After breakfast in their cells they were taken to a walled courtyard in the corner of the compound. The outer wall was so high they could see nothing but the tops of the trees and the roofs of a few houses outside. The inner walls were low enough for a guard to patrol on the other side, leaving them alone to stroll around in twos or threes, lapping up the warmth of the sun, gossiping. All the stories of ejection, capture, and interrogations came out.

Harish Sinhji had just missed landing on a tree, and his orange and white parachute had been caught there, like a sunburst, advertising his presence. He was considering hiding in a nearby cane field until dark when he looked up and saw thirty or forty people heading towards him. He ran for his life, heading into the cane, sweating like the devil until he realized he was still wearing his mask and helmet. Still on the run, he threw them off.

'But the crowd soon caught up with me. One chap was carrying an axe. I really thought I was a goner.' Some men in the crowd stopped the fellow with the axe, but others lit into Harry with their hands and feet. Then, suddenly, the frenzy stopped. Sinhji was blindfolded and his hands were tied behind his back. The military had arrived.

Tejwant Singh figured the villagers who got to him were angry because he was not carrying the usual issue of 200 Pakistani rupees plus revolver. (He didn't bother to carry the standard packet since he knew he had no chance of avoiding capture, not with his long hair and beard.) The first fellow who reached Singh ran off with his watch. The next one found his gutka (prayerbook) in the pocket of his G-suit and ran off with that. 'Those who were slower to reach me searched my pockets and found nothing so they took out their frustrations by beating me.'

When he saw two uniformed men holding .303 Lee-Enfield rifles from World War I, he begged them not to shoot. 'Don't worry,' said one of the guys, 'we're here to protect you.'

Soon a tonga arrived to take him to an army base, but before that a very strange thing happened. The fellow who'd stolen his gutka came back and returned it. 'Take this,' the man said. 'It'll come in handy.' And he was right, during his week in solitary confinement and even afterwards he found comfort in reading his gutka.

The only POW who hadn't ejected was Mulla-Feroze. He had been part of a Forward Air Control (FAC) team assigned to designate targets for the IAF. His team had been working along the border between Rajasthan and Sind. It was desert area where the front between the two armies shifted rapidly and somehow the Indian FAC team advanced behind enemy lines. When they came upon a column of vehicles kicking up the dust, Mulla-Feroze thought at first he was dealing with the Indian Army instead of an advance party of Pakistani troops. He walked over to the first jeep, thumped on its hood, and demanded to see an officer. The next thing he knew a jawan had shouldered his rifle, and when Feroze reached for his revolver, the man shot him through the arm.

Mulla-Feroze was a proud, impulsive fellow, and the incident seemed entirely in character. He was determined to keep the camp staff at arm's length—they were the enemy after all. But part of his edginess may have been caused by the pain of his wound. The flesh and most of the tricep had been blown away, baring the bone.

Bhargava's Marut had been shot down by ground fire on his first sortie. He, too, was captured in the desert of Sind, not far from the Rajasthan border. Shortly after 9.00 a.m. on 5 December, he landed on a sand dune and found himself alone, without a village in sight. He hid his G-suit in some shrubbery and changed his watch to Pakistan Standard Time. Then he took the compass from his survival pack and began to walk east. By noon he had finished the four small bottles of water from his survival pack. He was exhausted from climbing sand dunes and his back was killing him.

He was on the verge of giving up when he saw a large village ahead that he thought might be in Indian territory. He stopped at a farmer's hut just short of the village, introduced himself as a downed Pakistani pilot and asked for water. The farmer pointed to the cattle trough. Bhargava dipped one of his bottles and drank his fill.

'Can you tell me the name of that village?' he asked the farmer.

'It's Pirani Ki Par,' the man answered.

Bhargava realized then that he was still in Pakistan. But at least he now knew his exact location. Skirting the village, he set out in an optimistic mood, with his thirst quenched and his four water bottles full.

It was near dark when his luck ran out. He encountered three men who questioned him. Who are you, they wanted to know, what are you doing here? He stuck to the story that he was a downed Pakistani pilot, and said that his name was Flight Lieutenant Mansoor Ali. But the men were suspicious. They took him to a village and kept him there, sitting on a charpoy in someone's yard, until four rangers from the border patrol arrived to question him. Once again he repeated his story but they were not buying it either.

'Say the Kalma,' ordered one of the rangers. Every Muslim knows the Kalma (roughly translated 'There is no God but Allah and Mohammed is his messenger').

'I should have known the Kalma,' said Bhargava. 'I grew up in Pataudi, a princely state west of Delhi. Most of the people there were Muslim. But I couldn't remember the words and that was my undoing.'

The next morning Bhargava was handcuffed and blindfolded and set on a camel for a two-day journey to an army post. It was a painful experience, lurching along with an injured back. The halts were actually the worst part—getting down and up again was a real killer. 'I'd never been on a camel before,' he told his mates, 'and I don't recommend it.'

The men soon recovered from their beatings, all except for Vikram Pethia. 'Pethia had been so badly beaten up and manhandled by civilians as well as paramilitary forces that he could barely walk and couldn't eat properly,' remembers Grewal. 'He had fractured ribs and cigarette burns on his body. We helped him all day long, even supplementing his diet with an egg or two whenever we got one each. Our requests for a special diet and some medical help in the camp fell on deaf ears.'

The prisoners had a chance to air grievances and concerns when Mr B—, a representative of the International Committee of the Red Cross (ICRC), visited the camp. Once again the prisoners assembled in the interrogation room. They were very happy to meet Mr B—for he was the person who could confirm that they were registered as prisoners of war. This meant they were protected by the rules of the Geneva Conventions. It also meant that their families would be informed that they were alive and well.

The prisoners were impressed with Mr B—. They remember him as being a short, fair-haired man in his forties, probably Swiss, and very courteous. First he gave them a rundown of the history of the International Committee of the Red Cross and how it had helped prisoners of war ever since the South African war in 1899. He told them that before too long they would receive letters and parcels from home, though that could take a month or two. In the meantime, they could write letters and give them to the camp office. And every month, beginning immediately, they would be paid a POW allowance. The money could be used for purchasing personal effects, cigarettes, or food to supplement their diet. The amount of the allowance was prescribed by the ICRC, and depended on their rank, but he thought they would all find it adequate.

Pethia knew that he must tell Mr B—about his torture even if it meant subjecting all his comrades to the gruesome details. According to the Geneva Conventions all sick and wounded soldiers, including prisoners of war, must be treated humanely. Pakistan was a signatory of the Geneva Conventions, but in Pethia's case those rules had not been followed.

Pethia's Mystere had been shot down on 5 December. It was his fourth mission and the second day of the war. Like most of the others he had been robbed and beaten by villagers. That was par for the course. But unlike the others, his torment had not ended there. After suffering broken ribs from being beaten with rifle butts, he had been taken for interrogation to a room with high windows. The men who interrogated him were not dressed in uniform but he could tell from their questions and from the way they spoke to one another that they were military. When he refused to give anything beyond his name, rank and serial number, they burnt him with cigarettes. He was taken to the room more than once but he remained silent each time.

You have to give them something, thought Tejwant Singh. You have to make something up, change a few names, but you have to give them something. And then you have to remember what you've said, because they'll ask you the same questions again. Once on a training exercise he'd been dropped in 'enemy territory', then captured and interrogated. He too had refused to say anything except his name rank and serial number, but he'd been told in the debriefing that was a mistake.

Dilip thought of the fake sketches he'd made of the Adampur airfield. Had his shenanigans saved him? Or was it the luck of the draw? Perhaps he had simply encountered interrogators who were more humane than Pethia's.

At the end of the meeting, Mr B—read out the names of four pilots who were still missing and asked the POWs if they had heard anything at all about their whereabouts. All had been seen ejecting, but none had been reported among the dead or captured by the Pakistani authorities. Where were these men?

'Could you make some inquiries?' asked Mr B——. 'There's the staff here, and you may have some visitors from the air base. Do what you can.'

It was the worst moment of the meeting, even worse than hearing the details of Pethia's ordeal. Yes, they would do all they could to find out what had happened to these pilots, but they knew in advance their efforts would be futile. What would have happened to me, thought Dilip, if that policeman had not arrived in time? If the villagers had beaten me to death, would the authorities have returned my battered body to India? As for Pethia, all he could think was 'Why did they let me live?' It would have been very easy for his tormentors to kill him. Why did they let him live to tell his story? He had no trouble imagining what might have happened to the four men on the list.

Shortly after the visit of the Red Cross rep, the chief flight surgeon of the Pakistani Air Force visited the camp, probably at the urging of Dr Sarfraz, who had been attending the injured in their cells. As a result of the visit, all eleven ejection cases were sent to the Chaklala air base medical inspection (MI) room for x-rays and Mulla-Feroze was taken to a military hospital. After the medical assessments Kamat's broken legs were reset and Jafa was put in a body cast. Jafa and Singh had both suffered spinal injuries from their ejections and were prescribed bed rest. Along with Kamat, they spent the next two months in the MI Room. Chati, the youngest of the POWs, who had injured his jaw while ejecting, was sent to the MI Room for regular infrared treatments on his jaw and then to a dentist.

Bhargava's spinal injuries were deemed untreatable. He was inclined to blame his long walk in the desert followed by two days on a camel. 'Just don't bend over,' a doctor told him. 'Don't even tie your shoes.' He hoped that if he followed instructions, he might one day be able to fly again.

On their trips to the MI Room, the military hospital or the dentist, the POWs travelled in a van. They wore no blindfolds on these trips and it was a good opportunity to look around. They already knew that they were being held at No. 3 Provost and Security Flight in Rawalpindi. Now they could see that the flight's compound was located near Mall Road in the heart of the Rawalpindi cantonment.

There were actually a few signs in English, though most of them were in Urdu. But while all the POWs could understand spoken Urdu, which is very similar to Hindi, few of them could read it. After Partition, India's central government had ruled that the national language, Hindi (once called Hindi–Urdu), be written in Devanagari script rather than the Perso-Arabic script. Only Coelho and Jafa had learned to read Urdu at school, and that was over twenty years ago. Reading an Urdu street sign in passing was pretty well impossible.

But the POWs were familiar with the layout of cantonments. They had spent most of their careers living in similar enclaves. Cantonments had been built in British times to house the offices, barracks and bungalows of military personnel and their families. Rawalpindi, located near the turbulent northwest frontier, was the site of one of the largest cantonments in British India. Throughout India and Pakistan, the old cantonments continued to house military personnel. They were, for the most part, spacious, treed, residential suburbs and oases of calm and order compared to the older cities nearby.

In 1972 the new Pakistani capital, Islamabad, just north of the Chaklala air base, was still under construction. In the meantime, for all practical purposes, the Rawalpindi cantonment was the centre of power. It housed the president's residence as well as the headquarters of the Pakistani Army. Although the Indian POWs did not know it, they resided not far from Pakistan's president, Zulfikar Ali Bhutto, a man who would have a prime role in deciding their fate.

In January, Bhutto was beset with a number of problems. At the top of his list was the return of 93,000 Pakistani prisoners of war, but first the Bangladeshis insisted on formal recognition, and India (who was actually holding the prisoners) backed them. And now Bangladesh wanted to put some of the Pakistani prisoners on trial as war criminals. Bhutto had already appointed a judicial commission to get to the bottom of such allegations, but there was no way he could allow Pakistani officers to be tried as war criminals in Bangladesh without facing a military coup at home. No wonder he was suffering from insomnia.

Meanwhile, down the road, the Indian POWs used their medical outings through the cantonment to scout the lay of the land. Soon they had the route to the Chaklala base memorized. And they knew that Mall Road was also the Grand Trunk Highway, an ancient road that ran all the way from Calcutta to Peshawar. If you turned left onto Mall Road and kept going, you would eventually reach the Indian border. If you turned right you were on the road to Peshawar and beyond that to the Khyber Pass and Afghanistan.

The eight POWs who remained in the camp missed the company of their four comrades in hospital. Still, their mood was usually optimistic as they strolled around the courtyard, lapping up the sun. India had won the war. They had survived. In a matter of months, they would go home. One day they bet a bottle of beer on the date of their repatriation. Grewal, who considered himself a realist, bet on 29 May. The other bets ranged from March through April.

In January, as Mr B—had promised, each POW received the 'salary' due all POWs under Red Cross supervision. For the first month it amounted to Rs 57 for flight lieutenants, but none of the prisoners was paid the whole sum on the first payday. It turned out that all those cups of tea offered during interrogations had been totalled up and deducted from the pay cheque. And it wasn't just the prisoner's tea that had to be paid for, either. The cost of the interrogators' tea had been deducted as well! Even worse, Chati discovered that his whole salary had been wiped out by a few decent meals.

'What would you like?' the good cop interrogator had asked him one day.

'The rotis here are very tough,' Chati had replied. 'I have trouble chewing them.'

'How about some Chinese food?' the interrogator had suggested. So meals of noodles and rice were sent to his cell several days in a row, arousing the suspicions of Kuruvilla who was sharing a cell with Chati at the time.

'I didn't know why they'd put me in with you in the first place,' Kuru confessed. 'And when you got those special meals I became even more suspicious. Maybe this guy's a collaborator,

I thought, so I watched my words.'

When the first payday arrived and Kuruvilla discovered that Chati had paid for the meals himself, the air was cleared. In fact, everyone had a big laugh at Chati's expense. It turned out he had racked up such a big bill that he had overdrawn his allowance for the next two months.

They decided, since funds were scarce, to pool some of their money. Brother Bhargava became the keeper of the common purse. Their first order was a jar of pickle and large chunk of jaggery. Their meals, trucked in from the enlisted men's mess at Chaklala, were adequate but never tasty. A little pickle with the meal and a lump of jaggery afterwards, for the sweet, was a definite improvement.

Early in January, Dilip wrote a letter to his good friend, Major Inder Khanna. He was worried about Inder. He had last seen him in Amritsar right before the war. Years before they had both gone to a palm reader who had predicted Inder would receive a major injury at about this time in his life. Since his friend tended to be accident-prone at the best of times, Dilip was inclined to take the prediction more seriously than he normally would.

IAF Officers' POW Camp
Rawalpindi, Pakistan
9 Jan '72


Dear Inder and Pamma,

A very happy New Year to you both and Anju and Anu as well. The address in the right top corner says a great deal. It means your friend is safe and in fact virtually without injury and is just whiling his time away, while all the National and International forces use their pressures and counter-pressures to get us home. For our part we hope these forces yield results as soon as possible.

There are 12 of us at this camp. At first we were all together but now 4 of the bad medical cases have been transferred to hospital. The capture, handling, transfer, and questioning of the guys here will be the subject of an interesting conversation for us later on. It is not without its humourous side as well.

Life has been gradually improving especially since the ceasefire. For Xmas we were all allowed to meet each other for the first time. The two Christian officers got a priest and we all shared two lovely cakes. New Year's was also brought in with plenty of singsong, some streamers for decorations and extra good food. Since Xmas we spend all the daylight hours together out in the sun. It is wonderful in this cold Pindi winter. At dusk we return to my room, get a lovely fire going and chat away until dinner. As expectations of a POW camp go, the life is much better than we thought it would be . . .

Tolerable as life is one is very anxious to go home. The twin curses of this place are boredom and lack of news. The first we combat with chess, carrom, and occasionally a rubber of bridge. The latter has no solution, and we really have no idea of the post-war situation in either country.

We even get paid for this confinement at the very handsome rate of Rs 57 per month. This money goes a long way towards tea and supplementing the meals . . . Our Pakistani captors are very reasonable. We seem to have established a very decent relationship based on humane qualities.

Once again I do wish very hard that you have emerged thru this entire skirmish unscathed . . .

Y. affly

Dilip

It was a carefully written letter that managed to avoid any blackouts from the Pakistani censors. And though there was a great deal left out, what Dilip chose to say, and worded so judiciously, was substantially true. In late December he had been moved from his single cell to a larger room next to the interrogation room. It had been Jafa's cell originally but after Jafa was moved to the hospital the POWs began to call it Dilip's cell or 'the Indian tea club'. It was the fifth in a line of cells that began at the guardhouse by the gate, but its construction was much older than the first four cells and it was separated from them and the toilet by a narrow alley.

Every day at five o'clock, the eight POWs left the courtyard and assembled in Cell 5 for tea. The room had a fireplace that was lit occasionally for a few hours, and it was furnished with a table and chairs as well as the two charpoys. Soon it became the room where the prisoners ate all their meals. They even acquired a pet—a half-grown calico cat, very skinny. It was happy with any scrap of food they threw on the floor for it. They paid little attention to the cat but still it stuck around. 'You could say she adopted us,' remembers Dilip, 'and we were grateful.'

Cell 5 was by far the most desirable cell in the complex. It had not only a fireplace and a ceiling fan, but also a window, high up in one wall. At some point Dilip began to share the cell with

Chati who was one of the walking wounded. He might have had to share it with Pethia too, but Pethia was suspected of having TB. For several weeks he was put on a course of antibiotics and quarantined in his cell.

Dilip was still determined to escape, but for the moment his plans were not settled. He had had second thoughts about the hostage-taking idea. He realized that a scheme that had worked in the western world, where there seemed to be greater respect for human life, might not work for him in the present situation. He could run into someone along the way who was willing to shoot the hostage, and make short work of him as well. It didn't seem to be a plan destined for success.

In the meantime he had noticed that the wooden frame of the window in his cell was rotting and the mortar that held the frame was deteriorating as well. From what he could tell, the bars were set into the frame alone and didn't extend into the bricks above or below. He figured with a little work he might be able to dislodge the whole frame.

However, even if the window frame gave way and he made it over the wall and onto Mall Road, he would have to be miles away before his escape was discovered. All this would take time to prepare. And he would need a plan not only to escape detection as he broke out of the prison, but a route to reach the border. For that he would need a map.

# Peshawar
## (13 August 1972)

They reached Peshawar at about six, just as the sun was rising. So far, so good. They got off the bus soon after entering the city, before reaching the interstate bus station, and headed for another dhaba where they again ordered tea. The tea was served in a most remarkable porcelain pot. It had obviously been broken, possibly more than once, and then put together again with glue and brass strips. There it sat, like a relic in a museum, but still in use, and without a leak. All three of them were fascinated. If they had really been on a holiday, as they were pretending to be, the pot would have made the perfect souvenir.

But they couldn't linger long, not even long enough to finish the pot of tea. Soon their comrades in Rawalpindi would wake up and their absence would be noticed. They needed to find the road to Jamrud, and then a place to hide out for the rest of the day. From Peshawar to the Afghan border was over forty kilometres. They estimated it would take them at least two or three nights of walking. But first they would have to find their way out of Peshawar.

By the time they left the dhaba the city was on the move. Harry Sinhji remembers their shock at how many men toted guns. 'We walked along the road and noticed we were among the Pathans,' he recounts. 'More than half the adults we saw were carrying arms. There was an auto-rickshaw driver with a gun resting against his windshield. All these people wore a kind of cross-belt or bandolier for ammunition or cartridges. We were on the fringes of the wild Northwest Frontier Province, an area where the only law was tribal law—tribal Jirga as the locals call it—and one which even the British could not tame.'

They soon came upon an empty tonga and Grewal established a price for a ride to Jamrud Road. He remembers negotiating with the tongawala, a young man dressed in the white salwar kameez typical of the region, with a cloth wrapped around his neck because of the early morning air. Grewal sweated through the entire transaction. 'The tongawala turned out to be very inquisitive and while I sat with him in front he bombarded me with questions that I had a hard time answering.'

First of all, even before they boarded, the fellow wanted to know where on Jamrud Road they wanted to go, so Grewal told him they were looking for a particular newspaper office, but anywhere on the road would do—they had plenty of time. But the questions didn't stop there. They continued right through the ten-minute ride.

'Where have you come from,' the tongawala asked. ('Lahore,' said Grewal, as planned.)

'What time did you catch the bus there,' he asked next, and then, 'Why are you going to a newspaper office?' ('Looking for work,' said Grewal.)

'But it's a Sunday,' said the fellow, 'won't the office be closed?'

On and on it went. It was a great relief when they came to an intersection and the tongawala pointed to Jamrud Road.

At that point, the three climbed out, and Harry Sinjhi handed the fellow a five-rupee note. 'He looked at me and shocked us by saying in English, "No change," says Sinjhi. I smiled and, forgetting that we were job-hunting paupers, said, "Keep the change." Considering our looks and the short ride, this was a mistake.'

'The tongawala stood up. There was a big question mark writ large on his face. It was evident that he felt there was something fishy here. He asked us to put our gear back and climb in. He would take us wherever we wanted to go. We said it wasn't necessary, but he insisted. So we just walked away, while he stood there looking very puzzled.'

# The Map

For over a month, the POWs' wives and parents awaited news. All they had received were telegrams sent from air headquarters that read 'deeply regret to inform you that your husband/son . . . is reported missing in operations.' Then, a few days after the telegrams, came letters signed by Air Chief Marshall P.C. Lal: 'I am very sorry to learn that your husband/son . . . was reported missing . . . I can well imagine how anxious you must be about him . . . I shall of course keep you informed of any news we may get about him. In the meantime please accept my deepest sympathies.' Then the weeks passed and they heard nothing at all.

For Dilip's parents the first news of their son came from an unexpected source. About the middle of January his father's sister phoned from Beirut. 'I've just been told by a diplomat here that a Parulkar is a POW in Pakistan,' she said. 'That must be Dilip.' At that point his parents lit an oil lamp. They kept it going until Dilip was released.

A few days later the families of POWs received telegrams from the IAF saying: 'glad to inform you that the Indian Red Cross Society has now reported that your husband/son . . . is prisoner in Pakistan stop letter giving details in post.'

On 4 February the names of 576 Indian prisoners of war were published in the *Times of India*. When he read the lists, Dilip's old commanding officer, M.S. Bawa, turned to his wife and said, 'I know Parulkar is going to try to escape. I hope he doesn't get himself killed.'

Meanwhile, in Rawalpindi, the prisoners began their second month of days spent in the courtyard, strolling, chatting, and playing chess and bridge and carrom (crokinole). Mulla-Feroze had returned from hospital but Jafa and Singh and Kamat were still away and no one knew how they were doing or when they would return. It had been over a month since Mr B——'s visit but no letters had come, no news of the outside world at all. They had no idea if the Indian government was negotiating their release, or even an exchange of the sick and wounded, which they knew should come first.

On 26 January the POWs had celebrated India's Republic Day. It was the first break in their daily routine since the party on New Year's Eve. They used their pooled funds to order a good lunch and some sweets and fruit to distribute to the camp staff. Before lunch they sang the national anthem and observed two minutes of silence for their fallen comrades. Usman Hamid was invited to the function but he sent MWO Rizvi in his place. When they sang the national anthem, they were pleased to see that Rizvi stood respectfully at attention.

By February Pethia was out of quarantine though his

condition had not improved. It was good to have him back. He enjoyed a game of bridge above all else and served as the resident expert on the game. Four men would play while the others offered advice and cheered them on. The exchanges sometimes became very hot and some thought that the debriefings went on for far too long.

It was difficult to please everyone and even harder to remember the courtesies due to Coelho who was ten years older than the rest of them and had to spend all day long in the company of men of lower rank. For years it had been his job to train young pilots and teach them discipline and respect, but now circumstances were far from normal. The younger men should have addressed him as 'Sir'; they should have said: 'Please pass the salt, Sir,' or 'Goodnight, Sir,' but some of them dispensed with such courtesies or simply forgot them. When that happened, or if the banter became rough, Coelho would never say a word, but occasionally he would ask to be taken back to his cell and the younger officers would all know that he was displeased.

Boosting morale, maintaining physical and spiritual and mental fitness, were the challenges and they all knew it. Every morning they bathed in cold water. On a day that promised sun a man might wash his shirt, pants and underwear at the same time, wringing them as dry as possible before he wore the same damp garments for the day. Every morning before breakfast Kuru did push ups in his cell and Coelho read his Bible. Coelho also folded his trousers and placed them under his bottom blanket at night to preserve the crease.

Dilip and Grewal  organized competitive games to help

themselves and everyone else keep fit and in good spirits. The first game they proposed was seven tiles, a game they had all learned in childhood. It required little equipment, simply a stack of pottery shards or flat stones—whatever they could find—and a ball which they had a lascar buy from the market. They would form two teams of two or three men each and go at it hard. The first aim was to topple the stack by throwing the ball from a distance of about ten feet (they drew a line in the dirt), the second was to rebuild the stack while the opposing team fired the ball at you. It was a wild game, so wild and crazy that they couldn't play it for long, but it gave them many laughs. Pethia and Bhargava usually formed the cheering section. Bhargava still had to be careful or his back would spasm, and Pethia was not well enough to play. Later they acquired a cricket bat and began to play French cricket, a hybrid game designed for small spaces, and since their courtyard was too small even for that, they made further modifications.

There was lots of talk and joking while they sat around catching their breath or playing chess or bridge or carrom. At first it was all a novelty. They heard about Grewal's trip to Europe a year before the war. He had taken a long leave, flown to Athens, and backpacked around for three months. 'I tied my hair in a ponytail,' he told Dilip, 'and everyone thought I was a hippie.' Everyone had a few good stories, well rehearsed, but as the weeks passed there was really nothing new to say.

One afternoon while they were passing time in the courtyard, some young men peeped over the outer wall and initiated a conversation. 'How is life?' they asked. 'How do you pass your time?' The young men said they were members of the

Rawalpindi Club, whose grounds were nearby. They returned
the next day and tossed several packs of high-quality playing
cards over the wall. They explained that at the club a pack of
cards was discarded after every ten hands. The POWs never
saw the young men again and wondered if the camp staff had
put a stop to their visits.

Most days either Rizvi or Usman Hamid popped in to see
how they were doing. Rizvi tended to linger if a game of chess
was in progress. He obviously loved the game. He would
stand there watching and they could tell he was itching to play.
Usman Hamid was more inclined to tell a funny story to cheer
them up. One day he told them how he had gone to England
for training at Staff College. He remembered being given little
notice of his trip and regretting that he would miss the very
popular Indian movie, *Mughal-e-Azam*. It had just opened in
Pakistan at the time. Don't worry, his father had told him. It
will still be playing when you come back. And sure enough,
when he returned almost a year later, the film was still playing
at the same movie hall.

'I've always wanted to travel overland to Europe,' said Usman
another day.

'So have I!' Dilip said quickly, sensing a chink of opportunity.
'Grewal and I were thinking of a trip to the Olympics in Munich
this coming summer. I have an aunt in Lebanon and he has an
uncle in Egypt. We want to stop in both places along the way.'

And that was Dilip's excuse for asking Usman Hamid for a
map, a school atlas, to be precise. If he and Grewal had a school
atlas, they could plan their trip to the Munich Olympics. Surely
they would be repatriated before the summer. And planning their

trip would give them something to do in the meantime. That was the story he told Usman Hamid, but in fact it was not an overland trip to Europe he had in mind.

On one of those sunny winter afternoons, while strolling in the courtyard, Dilip whispered to the others that he intended to escape. He told them about the state of the window frame and said that he intended to work on it.

'You can't be serious,' said Mulla-Feroze. In the military hospital he had encountered some civilians who attacked him as soon as they realized he was an Indian POW. A guard was stationed at his door, not to keep Mulla-Feroze in, but to keep others out. Pethia had had a similar experience on one of his visits to the hospital. To escape would be madness. Even if you could avoid the police and military, there were hundreds—thousands—of angry civilians out there.

When Dilip told his friends he intended to get a map from Usman Hamid, he got the same reaction.

'You've got to be crazy,' they said. 'He'll never give you an atlas. He's the camp commandant, for heaven's sake! He's not a bloody idiot!' Getting a map from Usman Hamid became Dilip's first challenge. He was determined to get the map from Hamid and no one else.

'He just wants to plan an escape so he can boast about it later,' Mulla-Feroze told the others, and he wasn't the only doubter. 'No one took him seriously,' remembers Sinhji.

In fact there was one person who did take him seriously and that was his batchmate Brother Bhargava. Soft-hearted Bhargava, who knew Dilip better than anyone, was very worried that his daredevil friend would carry through his plans.

'Don't do it,' he begged Dilip. 'You'll get yourself killed!'

Usman didn't refuse to give Dilip a map (in fact he said he would, at the time), but he didn't produce one either. Each time he popped into the courtyard or the Indian tea club for a visit, Dilip would remind him in a jocular way, 'Ah, I see you've forgotten our atlas again. How will we ever be able to plan our trip?'

Sometime in February Dilip began work on the window in Cell 5. The window was located on a side wall and looked onto a narrow alley between two of the buildings on the compound. Across from the window were the toilet and the shower used by the POWs so it was easy to check the state of the mortar around the window on both sides of the wall. Dilip found that the mortar on the outside wall was in an even greater state of deterioration than on the inside.

At the end of the alley, just a few feet beyond the window, were several strands of barbed wire that separated the prison compound from the grounds of the recruiting office next door. During the day a number of airmen and civilian staff worked at the recruiting office and some parked their bicycles along the barbed wire fence, but after five the recruiting office compound was deserted. Dilip planned to head that way once he climbed out the window. He knew his timing would have to be perfect. In the prison compound there were always four armed guards on duty, one stationed in the guardhouse and three patrolling. He would have to scramble out the window and through the fence at a moment when all three patrolling guards' view of the alley was blocked. He was hoping to take advantage of a sandstorm. They were common enough in the dry months before the beginning of the monsoon rains.

And so his work began. In the interval between tea at five o'clock and dinner at seven thirty, while the others played cards or carrom or chess, Parulkar would stand with his back turned, as if looking out the window, pull out one of his eating utensils (either knife or fork), and work on dislodging the already crumbling mortar around the window frame. He carefully replaced the large chunks, but the smaller bits he ground under his feet. Below the window was a raised square of crumbling concrete, slightly sloped towards a drain in the wall. At one time the space had been used by Muslim staff for washing their feet and hands and heads before their daily prayers. Now it came in handy, for it was in such a state of deterioration that no one, not even the sweeper, would notice a little extra debris.

While Dilip worked on his window, the others pretended not to notice. They really didn't want to be implicated. The war was over. They were being treated decently. Why rock the boat? But no one except Bhargava tried to stop him.

Dilip began other preparations for escape. He used part of his allowance to buy dried fruits—raisins and apricots and dates—that he would take with him. He grew a beard, believing that would help him blend in with the local population. And he was picking up some words and phrases in Punjabi and Pashto. Hindi and Urdu and Punjabi are so closely related that communication in the prison was never a problem, but learning the local lingo was a matter of fitting in. When he broke out he

59

might have to ask directions or answer a question. He would have to watch his words very carefully.

As much as a map and a feasible escape route, what he really needed was a partner, preferably someone whose Punjabi was better than his own. Dilip, like his cellmate Chati, was from Maharashtra, and while he understood Punjabi and Urdu and could make himself understood, his accent might give him away. He needed someone else to do the talking. And that person would have to be very fit. They would have to walk all the way to the border, hiding in the daytime and walking by night. They couldn't risk taking public transport.

It hadn't taken Dilip long to decide that Grewal was the best candidate. He was one of the tallest prisoners and certainly the strongest, and he was a Punjabi. He could even pass, as far as his looks went, for a Pathan. Grewal was tall and fair, like the Pathans, and he had grey eyes from his English mother. Even though Dilip had not yet decided whether to head east to India or west to Afghanistan, he knew that if he chose Afghanistan he would have to pass through the Northwest Frontier Province and that was Pathan territory.

The more Dilip thought about it, the stronger was his belief that with Grewal along, the whole enterprise would have a much greater chance of success. But so far Grewal was as sceptical of the enterprise as all the others. No matter how much charm Dilip employed, Grewal stood firm. He saw the whole thing as a crazy idea. Surely, if they just sat tight, they'd be home by summer, in any case.

# Waiting

Late in February news came that the medical cases were to be repatriated. It was the first news of any sort and raised all their spirits. At the MI Room, Jafa, Kamat and Singh prepared to leave at a moment's notice. At the camp, Bhargava used some pooled cash for sweets to celebrate the departure of Mulla-Feroze, whose wounded arm had almost healed. The remaining POWs were happy for their colleagues and for themselves. Action was being taken. The 'national and international forces' that Dilip had mentioned in his letter to Inder Khanna were finally producing results. They knew that once the medical cases were repatriated, they would be next.

However, there were the usual glitches. Mulla-Feroze was taken to the airport four times. For some reason the first three flights were aborted. Then they learned that he had been the only airman repatriated and the other three were still in hospital. They debated why Mulla-Feroze had been exchanged and the others left behind. Could it be that the Pakistani authorities assumed Mulla-Feroze was Muslim because of his name? If so the joke was on them because he was actually a Parsi. Or perhaps they believed Mulla-Feroze, as a junior officer, was less of a threat to Pakistan? On the other hand, his wound had been serious, and when they met Mr B— in December, all the POWs had supported his repatriation on medical grounds. The repatriation of Mulla-Feroze, who was now in good shape, would remain a mystery. Like everything else in their present world, the decision was completely out of their hands.

The ICRC plane that took Mulla-Feroze home returned to Pakistan with the first batch of mail. When the Red Cross representative arrived at the camp, all the prisoners met him once again in the interrogation room. It was another man, not Mr B— and they were far more interested in getting their mail and parcels than they were in a long conflab.

When they were questioned about their treatment, they mentioned the obvious deficiencies of their camp: one toilet and shower for the lot of them, and the same tasteless food day after day, trucked in from the enlisted men's mess though they were all officers. But they admitted the camp staff were treating them decently and that the medical care had improved (though Pethia was still no better). They were all pleased when the rep told them that he believed the treatment of POWs, on both sides of the border, was the best he'd seen in any conflict.

'This can be used to your advantage,' he told them. 'When the authorities here know that their own prisoners are being treated well, they are more inclined to treat you in the same manner. We call this "simultaneous reciprocity".' It was a term they would remember and use later on.

After the formal part of the meeting, the Red Cross rep distributed the mail. They were disappointed to find that there were no parcels. Some of the POWs received four or five letters but Bhargava received none. He thought of his wife Anu and their two children waiting for him at home. What could have happened? Had there been some disaster and no one wanted to inform him? He was beside himself. 'You can read my letters if you like,' said Dilip. Grewal made the same offer, and Bhargava took them up on it.

Those who did receive letters found that all of them had been written before anyone had received their letters. All the news was more than a month old and some of the letters had sentences blacked out by the censor. Dilip received letters from his parents and sisters but nothing from his friend Inder Khanna. Shortly after the mail arrived, he wrote to Inder again.

IAF Officers POW Camp
Rawalpindi, Pakistan
7 Mar '72

Dear Inder and Pamma,

Last week we got our first batch of mail and was slightly disappointed not to find one from you . . . perhaps you did not receive the earlier letter which I wrote from here.

The mind goes back to the palmist and her rather gloomy forecast that you would be badly injured about this time in life. I for one have only believed the good things palmists have to say and rejected the rest. Consequently I do fervently hope that when we next meet, soon, we shall have a good laugh and scoff at miserable predictions.

Both '65 and '71 have been eventful years for yours truly. The chance of ending up in a POW camp had never crossed my mind but this is also a great experience as long as one does not make it a habit.

Life at this camp is better than tolerable. We spend the whole day from after breakfast to 5 p.m. in a small walled compound. The day passes playing carrom, chess, bridge—which I learned just before the Ops—we also have some lively games of 7 tiles and a little bit of non-hard-hitting cricket. The ball must not leave the compound.

The food is certainly adequate, in fact almost every single one of us has put on weight since we came here. We even had a tape recorder for a few days but it went out of order and we haven't seen it for almost a month.

Now that the first batch of mail has arrived we are all anxiously waiting for parcels to follow, and above all we all wait for news about repatriation. The other day some sick and wounded were exchanged. Only one pilot from this camp managed to get his name on that list and even as I write he is probably having himself a gala time in Delhi or Bombay. Now since that exchange has started could our turn possibly be far behind?

If one must look for advantage of this miserable period of our lives, it is in all the money lying accumulated in India. Here amongst us is a pilot who took furlough and hitchhiked around Europe last year. Both of us are crazy about physical fitness and games. As a

result we have decided to make it to the Munich Olympics together.
That would be the most befitting way to wash this bad taste out of
our mouths.

All the V Best to both

affly

Dilip

As usual, Dilip was inclined to focus on the positive and make
light of the negative. Usman Hamid had given them a tape
recorder and one tape on New Year's Eve. They had played the
tape over and over again until the recorder gave out a few weeks
later. Having some music had boosted their spirits for a while.
And now they had received their first letters with promises of
parcels to come. As for their IAF pay cheques accumulating
in their accounts at home, only the bachelors (Dilip, Grewal,
Chati, Sinjhi and Pethia) could expect a windfall. The other
POWs were married men. Barring any bureaucratic glitches,
their monthly pay cheques were being sent to their wives.

There was other good news but there was no way Dilip could
tell Inder about it in a letter. One day in mid-February, when
Usman Hamid dropped in to check on his charges, he tossed
Dilip an Oxford School Altas. 'To plan your trip,' he said. 'I'll
collect it in a week or so.'

But he never did collect the atlas. Soon after his visit Usman
Hamid was posted out. A little later they heard that he had
become an ADC to the Chief of Air Staff.

Many years later, when he read Sami Khan's *Three Presidents
and an Aid,* Dilip learned just how close to the centre Hamid
was during the early, uncertain days of Bhutto's presidency. On

3 March, after only a few weeks as ADC to Air Marshal Rahim Khan, Hamid and his boss were summoned to a meeting at Bhutto's residence, along with the chiefs of staff of the army and the navy. Bhutto had decided to clean house. While all the ADCs were kept closeted together in one office, Bhutto dismissed his army and air force chiefs and had them removed from the premises to secret locations. Then he swiftly made new appointments. The new air chief, Air Marshal Zafar Chaudhry, had been serving as the managing director of Pakistan International Airlines. Now he was suddenly at the top of the military hierarchy. Perhaps that's why he decided to keep Usman Hamid on as ADC.

After studying the Oxford Atlas's map of Pakistan and consulting the scale to measure distances, Dilip figured he should head northeast to Poonch. Poonch, the closest town in Indian-controlled Kashmir, was approximately 100 kilometres from Pindi, as the crow flies. He would have to cross the Jhelum River but it would be during the dry season (before June) so he didn't see that as a problem. What he really needed was a more detailed map of railways, roads and bridges, though he might have to avoid those in any case. He kept the atlas under the blankets on his charpoy for future reference.

Shortly after the departure of Mulla-Feroze and the arrival of the first mail, Jafa, Kamat and Tejwant Singh returned from their long sojourn at the Chaklala MI Room. It was good to have them back. Kuruvilla, who missed his meat and had ordered tinned meat several times through one of the lascars, now requested a bottle of whiskey. What arrived was not whiskey but Murree gin, which they used for their furtive celebration.

The compliant lascar's name was Aurangzeb. He was an elderly man, unshaven and generally careless about his appearance, but always obliging. The POWs liked to joke about their Aurangzeb, so different from the puritanical Mughul emperor Aurangzeb, who had once ruled India. Luckily their Aurangzeb was more flexible. A courageous chap, too, they thought, knowing the strict Islamic stance against liquor.

The POWs had been sorry to lose Usman Hamid and they never liked his replacement, Squadron Leader Wahid-ud-din. Wahid-ud-din was a tall, boisterous fellow with rough manners—'an I specialist', they called him because he was inclined to be boastful. When they learned he was a grounded pilot they had even less respect for him. One day, soon after the three came back from hospital, Wahid dropped in, and in the course of conversation referred to 'East Pakistan', which was now Bangladesh.

'Is the man talking in the past tense?' quipped Jafa, looking around at his colleagues.

Wahid was apoplectic with rage and threatened to put Jafa on charge. This incident was another strike against him, as far as the POWs were concerned, and there were more to come. When Wahid later told the prisoners that he was bringing members of his family to visit them, they were not pleased. 'We were being treated as a curiosity,' says Dilip. 'We felt like monkeys in a cage.'

They had had a few visits from PAF officers before this, including the commander of the Chaklala base. You could call them duty visits. Most of the PAF officers knew they could have been in the same boat themselves and might have appreciated having a few visitors to cheer them up.

67

'We may be enemies in the air,' one chap said, 'but we can be friends on the ground. If you ever need anything, let me know.' These turned out to be empty words, since the Indian POWs never saw the Pakistani officer again.

There was almost always a certain awkwardness in these visits, even from men of goodwill, for Pakistan had lost badly in the war and the superiority of the IAF had been an important factor. If the talk turned to history, that could be a minefield, too. The 1947 Partition of India had been a horror—they might all agree to that. If they went any further and tried to discuss the reasons for Partition or the responsibility for its results, they were soon mired in disagreements.

Jafa, Tejwant Singh and Bhargava enjoyed visits from Pakistani pilots they had trained with overseas. Singh and Bhargava had trained on the Sabre in the States, and Jafa had been to Staff College in the UK. No awkward conversations during these visits, just jokes and reminiscences about old times. The other POWs were there, too, in Cell 5, witnessing the fun. Jafa's friend came with his wife, who remarked that prisoner morale seemed high despite the difficult conditions. 'And Jafa,' she said,' I can see you haven't lost your charm.'

The pilot who had trained with Singh and Bhargava in the States came alone, but at the end of the visit he surprised everyone by announcing that his wife was waiting in a car outside. 'Since you are my brothers,' he told his two friends, 'please do me the honour of coming to meet her.' The corporal on duty agreed to the request and accompanied the two prisoners outside the gate. Everyone was aware that the PAF pilot, a strict Muslim, had done something exceptional to express his friendship.

At some point in March or April the new Air Chief, Zafar Chaudhry, paid a visit accompanied by his ADC, Squadron Leader Usman Hamid. It was an informal early morning affair with the two men visiting senior officers in their cells, but hurried as the visit was, those who received Chaudhry remember him as being genuinely concerned about their welfare.

The visit of Wahid's family, which the prisoners had dreaded, turned out to be one of the most memorable visits of all. It may have been in May or June. The weather had already warmed up. At teatime Wahid drove into the courtyard with his whole family in the car. From Cell 5, where the prisoners had assembled as usual, they saw two women and several children step out of the car. The door to the cell was unlocked and the visitors filed in. Wahid introduced the ladies as 'my wife and my sister-in-law'. The women were not veiled and were dressed in typical Punjabi salwar kameez. But no one was interested in the women's clothes, only in their lovely faces. The room was crowded and the visit did not last long but none of the prisoners has ever forgotten it. These were the first women and children they had seen in months and they found them all very beautiful. Two of the children were twin girls, maybe seven or eight years old.

After a few minutes one of the ladies began to weep. 'My brother was in the army and is a prisoner in India,' she told them. 'I wonder how they are looking after him?' The prisoners tried to assure her that the Pakistani POWs were being looked after very well, from what they had heard. 'Don't cry,' they told her. 'He will be fine.' After the family left the prisoners realized that maybe their appearance—rumpled clothes, some with beards, others unshaven (only a few of them took the trouble to shave on a regular basis), some wearing canvas shoes—had disturbed the woman. They didn't look like officers at all.

The next day Wahid arrived with a sumptuous lunch cooked by his wife and her sister. The attendants unloaded the containers from his car and set them on the table for everyone to share. For a few days after the feast they were inclined to think Wahid wasn't such a bad fellow.

Throughout March the POWs continued to spend all day in the courtyard. On occasion, when Wahid was absent, Rizvi would sit down and play a game of chess, and how he loved to win! Otherwise it was the same routine: a few energetic games of seven tiles followed by French cricket in the morning and cards or board games in the afternoon. Towards the end of March temperatures reached 30 degrees in the afternoons. A few POWs returned to their cells to nap or read but they all gathered for tea at five o'clock. After tea Dilip would stand at the window, his back to the door, as if looking out. He was making progress. He estimated the wall was at least 25 cm thick. He could already insert his knife up to the hilt in some spots. All he needed now was a little more work and a good sandstorm.

Some days, from the courtyard they could see children flying their kites from the roof of a building nearby. One day a kite floated into the courtyard. Its string had been cut in competition and both sides raced to retrieve it. Soon there was a pack of boys at the wall and one of the POWs reached up to hand the kite back. But that wasn't the end of the story. A few days later some boys brought a kite and spool to the wall so the POWs could fly one of their own kites. Jafa, who knew the Urdu script, wrote their address on it: No. 3 Provost & Security Flight, Mall Road.

For a few days the POWs had fun flying the kite in competition. When its string got cut, they heard it had been delivered back at the gate, but they never saw it again.

Another incident, one that no one who witnessed it will ever forget, happened in the courtyard one morning during a game of seven tiles. As usual Dilip threw himself into the game with great gusto. That morning, while trying to catch the ball, he crashed into a wall, then fell to the ground in a convulsion. 'His teeth got locked,' remembers Bhargava, 'and we all ran helter-skelter trying to do something to help him. We were scared sh**** seeing his condition. Kamat asked for a spoon which was immediately brought and he forcibly put it in Dilip's mouth. This carried on for some time and it had us all praying. Gradually he got back to normal and became his usual humourous self, asking why we had stopped playing. In fact he did not know what had happened.'

For a while they stopped playing seven tiles. The other POWs urged Dilip to see a doctor, but he refused. He soon felt well again, and he did not want a suspected seizure on his medical record. At the end of March he distributed all the dried fruits he had collected to take with him on his escape. He knew he wouldn't be leaving quite yet. In April he would receive the next 'pay cheque' and could always buy more.

# On the Road to Jamrud
## (13 August)

On and on they walked down the road from Peshawar to Jamrud, but still there were shops and shacks lining the road, and a constant stream of people who turned to look at them.

'What made things worse,' remembers Sinjhi, 'was that whatever they were doing, on spotting us they would stop their activity and stare intently at us. Several cyclists passed us, turned back, and passed us again . . .'

Just from their appearance it was clear that the trio were strangers. Almost every adult male they met along the road was dressed identically in a dirty white salwar and kurta. Each had a pale complexion, a dark beard, and a white cotton cap on his head. And here they were, such a motley crew. Grewal was wearing the salwar he'd had made from some frothy, turban material and he had wound a cloth carelessly around his head like a Punjabi farmer. Dilip wondered why he'd done that.

Though the sun was already hot, it was still a strange thing to do. But then Grewal was a Sikh. Maybe he felt uncomfortable in public without something on his head. Possibly it was Dilip himself, with his darker complexion, who was attracting the unwanted attention. Or maybe it was the slightly built Harry Sinhji, dressed in western clothes, with a moustache but no beard. Or could it be that men of their class would never be caught dead walking down the road from Peshawar to Jamrud? Men on excursions from other parts of Pakistan, unbearded men sporting moustaches, or even fedoras, might drive through the area, but would they ever think of walking?

Yes, so few strangers travelled Jamrud Road on foot, they were bound to be noticed. When they look back on that morning, they realize that they were objects of a very natural curiosity, probably nothing more, but at the time, each question, each look, was a searchlight, a beacon, not of hope but of imminent capture. If a tongawala and a boy on a bicycle were suspicious enough to question them ('What's in your bag?' a boy asked Harry Sinhji on Jamrud Road), what would happen if they encountered an official?

Before long the pedestrian traffic thinned out, but there was still the odd cyclist as well as a gang of men working on the road. The three friends skirted heaps of gravel and walked straight on, past men loading basins, past other men with picks and shovels, past a truck spreading hot bitumen. They kept their eyes on the horizon, ignoring all the stares.

When they passed the Peshawar airfield they could see a runway quite near the road. 'Don't look,' warned Grewal. Against all their natural inclinations as airmen, they immediately averted their eyes.

As far as they could see, there was nowhere to hide. The land was a flat gravelly plain, no fields of sugar cane, little vegetation of any sort. It was altogether a barren place. After a mile or so, Harry Sinhji grew tired and lagged behind the other two but it wasn't such a bad thing after all because the group of three had attracted even more attention. And if the alarm had already gone up, as they believed, wouldn't the police be looking for a threesome?

# False Start

Early in April an ICRC rep arrived with a second batch of mail. This time he brought parcels and a volleyball net as well. Each POW received one parcel packed by the IAF which contained much-needed underwear, socks and night suits as well as toothpaste, razors, soap, needles and thread. Both Singh and Grewal received a length of cloth for a turban, but that was as far as customization went. The POWs were disappointed when they discovered that all the underwear was a small size. To much amusement, Kamat, with his few extra pounds, demonstrated the impossibility of donning the undersized shorts.

Some of the POWs received parcels from family as well. Families had been told they were allowed to send cigarettes and food, but no clothing apart from underwear. Nevertheless, Dilip's sister in Delhi, after reading his first letter about the cold, sent him a plush blue lounging suit. This was another cause for laughter. 'Where does she think I'm putting up?' he said. 'At the Ritz?' He put the suit back in the box and tucked it under his charpoy.

April saw the prisoners' acquisition of a radio, too. Somehow they had learned that Pakistani POWs in India were broadcasting greetings to their families in Pakistan. A chap would come on the air, say his name, greet his family, and basically tell them he was in good health. He might add a few details about life in his camp. The whole thing was actually a public relations exercise by India to show that it was treating its prisoners well. What interested our friends in Rawalpindi was the news that some Pakistani prisoners were listening to Hindi music all day long. It was piped into their camps through loudspeakers.

How they learned this news, no one remembers for sure. It could have come from one of the friendly camp staff, possibly Corporal Mefooz Khan, a tall Pathan. He wasn't the sharpest tack in the box but at least he was kind and he treated them with respect. Or maybe they deciphered the news themselves. Whenever the prisoners ordered chapli kababs from a dhaba nearby they would come wrapped in newspaper, always an Urdu newspaper unfortunately. But Jafa and Coelho, who had both studied Urdu, would sit down together and try to make sense of it.

However the inmates of No. 3 Provost and Security Flight learned that the Pakistani POWs had access to music, they decided to put this information to good use—they demanded equal treatment, 'simultaneous reciprocity', as they had learned this was called from the Red Cross rep. For twelve people a loudspeaker was out of the question, but Wahid-ud-din agreed to give them a radio. It was a transistor radio that needed many batteries, but as long as they could keep it going they were allowed to listen to anything they wanted to, even the BBC and All India Radio. It was a great morale booster.

Thus they learned that there were 93,000 Pakistani POWs in India, but only 600 Indian POWs in Pakistan, and that Zulfikar Ali Bhutto had replaced Yahya Khan as president. They could tell that, in Pakistan at least, pressure for an exchange of prisoners was strong. Bhutto had recently proposed a prisoner exchange in return for recognizing Bangladesh. There were rumours that high-level talks would take place before the end of April. All this was good news. It seemed possible that Grewal would win his bet and they would all be home by the end of May.

The radio newscasts provided other opportunities. When Tejwant Singh learned that thousands of Sikhs from around the world were coming to Gurudwara Punja Sahib, a Sikh shrine in Pakistan, to celebrate the spring festival Baisakhi, he had an idea. Why not ask Wahid-ud-din to allow him and Grewal to make the pilgrimage as well? The shrine was not far from Pindi, and since Muslims were inclined to take religious matters seriously, he thought he had a chance of success. Gurudwara Punja Sahib is 48 kilometres from Rawalpindi, in the foothills of the Himalayas. It is one of the holiest places of Sikhism because of the presence of a rock believed to have the handprint of Guru Nanak, the founder of Sikhism.

After some negotiation, Wahid-ud-din agreed to arrange for the trip, but it had to be a week or so after Baisakhi (13 April) so they wouldn't encounter crowds. He also agreed to let Jafa go along, though he was suspicious of Jafa's Sikh roots since he maintained a clean shave. (In fact, Jafa's father was Sikh and his mother Hindu, so both religions were practised in his family.)

The threesome left one morning right after breakfast, accompanied by four guards. The POWs were seated in one jeep with another jeep trailing. It was a short trip. The jeeps turned right out of the gate, then right again onto Mall Road and headed west towards Peshawar. The POWs noticed that Pindi was not a very big city on its western side.

Soon they were out of the cantonment. To the north they could see the foothills of the Himalayas and beyond them higher mountain ranges were faintly visible. Ahead, the road cut between two hills. This was the Margalla Pass. Once over the pass the jeeps dipped into a scenic valley and before long they turned onto a narrow road that led to the gates of the gurudwara.

The nineteenth-century gurudwara was an impressively ornate building that seemed to have been freshly painted for Baisakhi. At the gate they were greeted by three men who took them on a tour. The highlight of the tour was the rock with Guru Nanak's handprint set in the midst of a flowing stream of water. According to the story, when the guru touched the rock, a stream sprang forth to quench the thirst of his followers.

The jeeps returned to camp by lunchtime. Wahid-ud-din was pleased that he had done yet another good turn to raise the morale of his prisoners. Later, after the breakout, he was to change his mind about the expedition and accuse Jafa of using the outing to scout the lay of the land. He was wrong. At this point the escape project was still Dilip's alone.

Towards the end of April, the camp routine altered with the

rising temperatures. The prisoners began to spend most of their time in Cell 5, which had a ceiling fan. After breakfast they still strolled in the courtyard or played a few games of French cricket or seven tiles, but by mid-morning, with temperatures already in the 30s, they retreated to Cell 5 for cards, board games or reading. After tea at five, they played volleyball in the main yard. Then it was dinner at 7.30 and sometimes more cards or chess until everyone returned to their cells for lights out.

That was another change in routine. With the advent of warm weather the outer cell doors were left open at night to provide some ventilation. Since the lights from the yard allowed the guards to check on the prisoners, there was no longer any reason to keep cell lights on throughout the night. For over four months they had all struggled to sleep with the lights on. It was a great relief when they were turned off. But now there was the heat to contend with. Only Cell 5 was equipped with a fan.

Grewal had discovered that one of the civilian staff at the camp had once been a tailor and continued to do sewing after hours. Since he had given up wearing a turban for the duration of his stay in Rawalpindi, he used the turban material he'd been given in his parcel to have a salwar stitched. It was cooler than the serge pants they'd been issued and he started to wear it every evening. Dilip went one step further. He sent the obliging Aurangzeb to the bazaar to fetch material for a full suit. He, too, began to wear his green salwar kurta in the evening. The guards and attendants seemed pleased to see the POWs adopt some of their customs. And it was understandable that a man would want a change of clothes—something more comfortable, especially in the hot weather. Of course Dilip's real reason for acquiring the salwar kurta was to wear it the night of his escape.

By this time he had acquired not only the Oxford School Atlas, but also a pair of scissors for trimming his beard and a screwdriver for fixing the transistor radio. With these tools his work on the window picked up. Then, one afternoon, a group of workmen appeared carrying trowels and buckets. They had come to repair the drain trough that led from the washing platform under the window in Cell 5. The prisoners watched nervously as they went to work. Luckily none of the workmen noticed the loose window frame even though it was staring them in the face. They had been sent to do one job and that was it.

When the cement dried, Dilip could stand once again at the window that looked over the alley, but at first he could not dispose of debris by scuffing it around on the floor below. Then, after a week or so, the new cement, obviously poor quality stuff, began to crumble. When MWO Rizvi came to watch the chess players, Bhargava couldn't resist pointing out the poor quality of the work and the materials. Rizvi immediately went to examine the spot, and he didn't miss the loose window frame. He summoned a workman immediately and had him hammer nails into the frame to secure it. The next morning a crew of workmen were back with trowels and buckets of cement. They repaired the drain trough again and regrouted the window. This time they did a stellar job.

Bhargava was mortified. Though he had begged Dilip to give up his escape plan, he'd had no intention of sabotaging it.

'Bhargava was more upset than I was,' remembers Dilip. 'He couldn't stop apologizing. I just thought, what the hell, I'll have to find another way.'

He thought of lines from his favourite poem, Rudyard Kipling's *If*. At the National Defence Academy each cadet had a writing table and over that writing table hung a framed copy of *If*. For three years he had studied those stanzas and tried to apply them to his own life. He didn't find their message much different from the Gita. Both works were about duty and detachment and being your own man.

> If you can trust yourself when all men doubt you . . .
> If you can wait and not be tired of waiting . . .
> If you can meet with Triumph and Disaster
> And treat those two imposters just the same . . .

Success and failure—he was determined to take each one in his stride. No, he would not give up. He was surrounded by men who thought he was a fool, but he would not give up. He would find another way.

After Rizvi discovered that the window was about to give, he was on the alert for weeks. Bhargava had to work hard to make up for his faux pas. Whenever Rizvi mentioned the window, Bhargava tried to assure him that all was well: 'We are all comfortable here,' he would say. 'Why would we want to try such a thing?'

For the moment Dilip had to lie low. What he had in mind was a tunnel. If it ran under the back wall of his cell into the recruiting office compound, the tunnel would not have to be long or deep, just a dip under the wall. But now was not the time. He would have to wait. He was still on his own. No one else was interested.

Through most of April the prisoners' hopes were high that a prisoner exchange would take place very soon. On 20 April a newscast announced that high level talks would begin on 26 April at Murree, a hill station not far from Pindi. As scheduled, the talks went on for three days, behind closed doors. Pakistan was represented by its Secretary General of Foreign Affairs, and India, by Indira Gandhi's special envoy, D.P. Dhar. But the outcome of the talks was not encouraging. All that had been accomplished was setting a tentative agenda for further talks to take place between Gandhi and Bhutto in India. With this news the POWs knew that they would have at least several more months to wait for repatriation. By then they would have been prisoners for over six months.

'We realized,' says Dilip, 'that our fate was uppermost only in our own minds, certainly not in the minds of the politicians.'

The politicians, indeed, had a great deal on their minds, and having three countries' politicians involved complicated matters even further. One after another, countries in the Soviet Block and then in the British Commonwealth had recognized the independent nation of Bangladesh, prompting Pakistan to withdraw from the Commonwealth. Then in April Pakistan's ally, the United States, reluctantly extended recognition. Still Pakistan held out.

Sheikh Mujib Rahman had clearly refused to approve the return of the 93,000 prisoners of war until Bhutto agreed to recognition, but Pakistan had very little power in the negotiations ahead and seemed determined to hang on as long as possible to the carrot of recognizing Bangladeshi independence. Always lurking in the background (and occasionally in the foreground) was the Sheikh's determination to try some of the Pakistani POWs as war criminals.

For the POWs in Rawalpindi, the only good news was that summer came early in May. Finally Pethia was to be repatriated for medical reasons. As they had done to celebrate the departure of Mulla-Feroze, the POWs chipped in to buy sweets from a shop on Mall Road. Pethia was repatriated on 8 May, after five months and three days' imprisonment.

Now they were ten. Ten men who spent most of the day in a room with three charpoys, a table and chairs (most of them the chairs they carried to and from their cells each day), and a ceiling fan. They took turns playing bridge. They took turns lying down. The readers read whatever books that Rizvi fetched from the Chaklala base library. The books ranged from Dickens and Orwell to *National Geographic* but none was new. Jafa made notes from his reading in a school notebook. Singh began to keep a diary on onion-skin paper. After he'd made an entry he would store his wad of notes in the heel of his shoe. Both Singh and Coelho drew sketches of their fellow inmates and any members of the camp staff who they found interesting subjects. Still, no matter what anyone did, time weighed heavily.

It was a discouraging time, not only for Dilip with his escape plans on hold, but for the other prisoners, too. All their ways of keeping up morale: the volleyball competitions, the games of chess and bridge, the system of bridge winners buying treats for tea once a month when their pay packets arrived, the once-a-month possibility of letters, their growing links to a few friendly guards and attendants and even the cat who wandered into the tea club for tidbits and the occasional saucer of milk—all this was becoming stale and burdensome.   As time went on and nothing changed, it was an effort to maintain good temper and cheerfulness.  They had done their best for almost six months, but by mid-May, with temperatures rising daily and still no date set for a summit meeting between Bhutto and Gandhi, everyone's patience was wearing thin.

It was under these circumstances that Grewal finally capitulated. 'I'm in,' he told Dilip one day. 'But we don't need a tunnel. We can go through a wall.  I know how these old havelis are built. When my father was a magistrate in Punjab, two prisoners broke out of a place like this. They did all the work in one night.'

Dilip was elated. He had the very best partner he could imagine, the one he had been seeking for months. And he knew that once Grewal had given his word, he would never go back on it. He was a man with a great deal of pride.

# Grewal

Flight Lieutenant M.S. Grewal had been shot down on 4 December, the first day of the war. He may have been the first Indian pilot shot down or, at least, the first who was able to face the news media. Jafa and Chati came down the same day, but neither was available for interviews. Jafa had damaged his spine on landing. Chati had injured both his arm and face during ejection and was of no use for propaganda purposes.

It was Grewal's second sortie of the day, flying from Amritsar with the 32nd Squadron. In the first mission, he and his mates had successfully bombed an airfield, destroying a few grounded planes and airfield installations. That morning all of the 32nd Squadron's missions were successful and all pilots had returned safely. In the afternoon, they were assigned new targets. Grewal and his mates were to hit Rafiqi Airbase, which is southwest of Lahore near a town called Shorkot Road.

'Once again we took off, heading towards Pakistan, flying very low towards our target,' remembers Grewal. 'During our run-in, from the initial position to the pull-out point, we faced heavy flak. Being the number four in the formation, I saw the other three pull up safely. As I was rolling in to carry out my attack, I got hit by anti-aircraft artillery, lost control of my plane and ejected safely.'

Like Dilip, Grewal was immediately surrounded by villagers who took his watch and other valuables and beat him. But since he had landed about a mile from the airbase, the military police were soon on the scene. He, too, was blindfolded and taken on a long overnight trip in an open jeep to Rawalpindi. After a short stay in a cell, he was taken, sleepless, to a press conference where he was questioned by reporters for various news channels, as well as senior PAF officers.

'Having noticed prominent news channels such as the BBC,' says Grewal, 'I was confident that my whereabouts and condition would be known back home and everywhere else. In fact, I found out later that my friends and family in the US and Canada saw me on TV.' Most of India had no TV network at this point, but since Lahore's transmission could be well received in border areas, his father in Amritsar soon heard that someone had seen his son on TV.

And so began Grewal's incarceration, a time that eventually became so boring that he was willing to risk a breakout. For about ten days he was alone and very cold. His flying overall had been taken away and he wore only pants and a shirt. During the night he could hear bombs exploding and ack-ack fire, indicating that the war was still on.

During the day he would be taken for interrogation and two or three times he'd stood all night in a corner of the interrogation room because he had refused to answer certain questions. His guard, unlike the one assigned to Dilip, did not give him a break, and in the morning, when he was asked if he wanted tea, he said yes but the tea never arrived.

He remembers well being questioned by Chuck Yeager. 'This is not an interrogation,' Yeager began. 'I just want to ask you a few questions.'

When Yaeger told Grewal his name, he was surprised that he didn't recognize it. 'I'm the man who broke the sound barrier,' he said. 'You're a fighter pilot. You should know that.' Grewal thought the sound barrier had been broken by a British pilot called John Derry, but he knew enough to keep his mouth shut about that.

Yeager was interested mainly in the Sukhoi's fuel capacity and range. 'How did you get so far?' he asked, and 'How well do the ejection seats work?'

'Well, I'm here,' Grewal remembers answering, 'so they obviously work pretty well.'

Unlike Dilip, Grewal had had no childhood interest in flying. He had a most unusual family history, with many bumps along the way. He was born in Sheffield in 1942. His father had gone to England to study metallurgy before World War II. 'He went to study metallurgy but got involved in matrimony,' jokes Grewal. By the time the Grewals returned to India with their three young sons, it was 1947, just months before the partition of the country into India and Pakistan. They soon had to flee their home in Lahore and find a place for themselves in India. Grewal's father found work in Indian Punjab, first in Ferozpur, and then in Patiala, but by the time they were settled, his English mother had had enough. She left India in 1950 never to return.

Grewal owed his flying career to an uncle whose blue IAF uniform impressed him, and to the discovery of his somewhat latent talents. Although he had never done very well in school, in 1961 he sat for the Union Public Service Commission (UPSC) exams, without much hope, and he passed. When he passed the interview as well, he began training at the Air Force Academy in Jodhpur. 'At the time I couldn't ride a bicycle without having an accident,' he remembers. 'My father said, "How are you ever going to fly a plane?" But I did!' By 1971 he had been flying almost ten years and had gained a lot of confidence as well as competence.

On 16 December 1971, after ten days of solitary confinement, Grewal was taken outside without a blindfold and allowed to sit in the sun with Flight Lieutenant Harish Sinhji and Flying Officer Kuruvilla. He was meeting both men for the first time. In the next few days he met the others and realized that he was, indeed, one of the lucky ones. In fact other POWs remember Grewal as the strongest and the fittest, a natural partner for Dilip Parulkar in his plan to escape.

Why had Grewal resisted the idea of escape for so long and then changed his mind? This is the way he remembers it: 'By now it was May–June in the Indian subcontinent. The days were long and hot with very little news from home about our repatriation. Life started to get very intense and boring.'

Over the next few days Grewal and Dilip confided their plan to their senior officers, Jafa and Coelho. Coelho believed that having highly trained pilots risk their lives in an attempt to escape was very foolish, but since he could not really argue against a POW's well-known duty to escape, he hesitated to issue the order that would have stopped them. Jafa, on the other hand, realized that Dilip, and now Grewal, were hell-bent on the breakout and saw his role as facilitator. Careful preparation would be essential and he was willing to help.

The discussions began. Not everyone approved, but all were in on the planning, and each had his say. Should they head for India or Afghanistan? What supplies would they need for their trek? How, day after day, could they conceal their preparations from the thirty-five to forty guards who lived on the compound and patrolled around the clock? And who, in the end, should go? Harish Sinjhi was soon itching to be part of the team, but was he strong enough for the journey? These were all vital issues. The camp was abuzz. No one could say it was boring now.

Finally, on 27 May, Radio Pakistan announced that Bhutto would fly to Delhi on 28 June for summit talks with Gandhi. Once again hopes for repatriation rose, but this time Dilip and Grewal did not wait idly. They were determined to have their backup plan ready. If the summit failed to promise repatriation that summer, they would be off.

Meanwhile, northern India and Pakistan experienced the hottest June in years. As the prisoners sweated through the long hot days before the monsoon rains began, one of the first questions to settle was the escape route. If two prisoners could dismantle a section of wall overnight, there was no point in starting that part of the operation yet. The first thing to decide was their ultimate destination. Should they head east to India or west to Afghanistan?

India was certainly much closer. The Indian city of Poonch

was only 100 kilometres northeast of Rawalpindi. If they headed for Poonch, which was Dilip's original plan, they would now have to cross the Jhelum River during the monsoon. But if they headed west to Afghanistan, the border was more than twice as far, and they would have to cross the Indus. Whichever direction they took, they would have to skirt bridges and other possible checkpoints. The plan was to walk at night and hide during the day. They could reach the border near Poonch in three nights but reaching the Khyber Pass would take much longer. Even if they managed to avoid highways and bridges, the longer they were on the road, the more likely they were to be caught.

Of course, the authorities would expect them to head for India, but that wasn't the only problem with destination Poonch. Jammu and Kashmir, where Poonch is located, had been disputed territory since India and Pakistan gained their independence in 1947. After three wars, the line of control there was heavily fortified. They could step on a landmine. They could be shot by their own troops.

The Afghan border was peaceful by comparison. Once they reached Peshawar they would have to cross through Pakistan's Northwest Frontier Province to reach the border, and that was a notoriously lawless place. But they were sure they could count on a warm reception in Afghanistan. The Soviet-backed government of Afghanistan was on good terms with India. Seven years later, civil war would break out between the Afghan government and the US-backed mujahideen (which would go on to form the Taliban). But in 1972 Afghanistan was at peace. In 1970 Grewal had flown to Kabul and then on to Tehran and Athens.

All these factors were weighed by the members of the Indian

tea club, as they sat on charpoys indoors or played volleyball at sunset. At first Dilip and Grewal favoured Poonch but eventually they were persuaded to go west to Peshawar and the Khyber Pass. As for Harish Sinhji, he was a slight fellow and he didn't know how to swim, so they were reluctant to take him.

# Scrounging

When Grewal made his decision to team up with Dilip, he used some excuse (now forgotten) to ask for a shift to Cell 5. By this time some of the POWs liked to linger there longer than others each evening, playing cards or chess. Why not accommodate the players by letting them bunk together? It seems likely that MWO Rizvi's suspicions about the window had evaporated. It is even possible that he had not informed Wahid-ud-din about them in the first place. Or perhaps both men thought that with the Simla talks a month away, and a prisoner exchange likely to follow, they could relax.

So by June there were three men in Cell 5, and though Chati was there somewhat by chance, his presence proved to be useful. Because of his injuries, he could request visits to the dental clinic or the hospital and, along the way, scout the lay of the land. Dilip and Grewal, who were known for their fitness, did not have an excuse to leave the camp, and they needed all the information they could get.

They figured there was no need to start on the wall until a week or ten days before the escape, but in the meantime they needed to scout the premises and plan the route out. They quickly agreed that the back wall of Cell 5 was the best place for the breakout. Since that wall faced the same direction as the back wall of the bathroom, and since the bathroom had a ventilator, they were able to observe the PAF recruiting station and petrol pump behind their compound. The two compounds were separated by a barbed wire fence, about a foot from the back wall of the prison compound. Although the fence was high, it was not much of a barrier. They had observed airmen step through it to reach the recruiting compound.

By watching through the ventilator in the bathroom, they discovered that after five in the evening only a single watchman stood guard in the recruiting station compound. He sometimes sat on a charpoy, not far from the barbed wire fence, but when he did, he usually faced the other way, towards the gate on Mall Road. If they were quiet and quick, they could escape his notice. If he turned around they would be finished. It would be up to each man to check the watchman's position before making a dash across the alleyway and along the back wall of the other prison cells. As they neared the outer wall, the one they would have to climb over, the guard's view would be blocked by a hut on the recruiting compound. It was really the first twenty feet that were risky.

Once over the wall they would be on a side road, close to its intersection with Mall Road, which they knew was also the Grand Trunk Highway. If they turned right at Mall Road, they would be on the way to Peshawar and the Khyber Pass, but they couldn't risk travelling such an obvious route, even at night. They would have to go overland, avoiding the main roads, the big towns. They would need a compass, some food to keep them going, and at least a small supply of water. A ground sheet of some sort for sleeping on would come in handy, something to protect them from ants, and in the mountains, from the cold (though cold was hard to imagine at the moment). And a length of rope was always a good thing to have.

All of them had taken survival training in the air force. They had been dropped in the desert or the jungle or the mountains (usually all three) with just a compass, first aid kit, some matches, and a few flares, the same paraphernalia contained in the small cloth bag that accompanied them on all their flights, in case of ejection. But not one of them had managed to keep his survival kit. They had been stripped of everything remotely valuable either by the crowds that greeted them or by the military police. Only Chati's parachute and Coelho's anti-gravity suit were still on the premises. Coelho kept his G-suit in his cell. The parachute was stored in the cell by the guardhouse that had once belonged to Pethia. Since his departure that cell was used to store the surplus Red Cross boxes, most of them empty but a few of them still containing remnants of the latest delivery. Brother Bhargava had taken charge of the cell and kept the key. Though he needed permission to come and go, the guards were always obliging. Sometimes they were rewarded with leftover sweets or canned goods that had been sent to the prisoners.

Once Dilip and Grewal had taken stock, preparations began in earnest. There was a long list of things to do. They had to create their own survival kits, gather their own intelligence, and make plans step by step.

Devising a compass fell to Kamat who knew the most about physics. He used scrounged wire and cells from the transistor radio to magnetize a sewing needle. For a pivot he used the hollow half of a press button (the type of snap button used on all the shirts they had been issued), and mounted the pivot on yet another sewing needle so that the pivot could swing freely. Using as a model the compass rose from the Oxford School Atlas, Coelho drew a new compass rose on letter paper. When that was ready, Kamy pushed the base sewing needle through the rose's centre for another test and the whole apparatus proved true. Then he took the whole thing apart, wrapped the pieces in cotton batting, and stuffed them into a hollowed out biro pen that Dilip could carry in his pocket when the time came.

Other things fell into place in strange, serendipitous ways. For weeks the volleyball net had been useless because of a broken rope. After repeated requests for rope, all falling on deaf ears, the prisoners had given up. Now someone suggested replacing the broken volleyball rope with the rope from Chati's parachute. They could use part of the rope to fix the volleyball net, and keep another length for the survival kits. With permission, Bhargava fetched the blood-stained parachute from the dump cell. When he returned it, the parachute was missing not only its lines, but a good chunk of its many yards of fabric. They had cut lengths of its yellow and white nylon for groundsheets. The fabric was light and folded to a pack that would fit the palm of your hand.

It was strong, too, and if it hadn't been such a bright colour, they could have used it to make knapsacks.

That was a problem, or one of the many problems. How were they to carry everything? Grewal and Dilip had already decided to pose as PAF airmen on leave, off for a hike in the mountains. Knapsacks would be ideal but, even if they had enough cash, they couldn't send Aurangzeb to the market to buy knapsacks.

It was around this time that the POWs' good luck blossomed and several important pieces of the puzzle fell into place, one after the other. On 11 May the Pakistani rupee was devalued from five rupees to the American dollar to eleven rupees. When the prisoners received their pay packets in June, the flight lieutenants found that their salaries had increased from 57 rupees per month to 147. 'Surely the fastest pay rise in history,' jokes Dilip.

Bhargava remembers celebrating by ordering Chinese food from Hotel Flashman, which was near the camp. 'In fact we became regular customers and we particularly enjoyed pastries from there which we normally had after the game of volleyball.' Despite these extravagances, the rise in POW allowances still allowed more cash for the escape. They would have enough money to take a bus, hire a tonga or even a taxi. They could stop at a tea stall to eat. They could behave, in other words, like any other travellers on holiday, though they would still have to be prepared for long hikes over rough, wild territory.

The idea of taking a bus was farfetched until Dilip discovered, by accident, that in Rawalpindi there were buses arriving and leaving right through the night. One day he was talking to a Pathan guard, trying to learn something about the northwest frontier. 'Where is your village?' he asked. 'How often do you get leave? How do you get home?' The guard told him that he could finish his shift and catch a bus that very night to Peshawar. Dilip knew that Peshawar was only about fifty kilometres from the Afghan border. It was a major centre and therefore a place to be avoided, but if they arrived in the early morning, perhaps they could be out again before arousing suspicions. Hopping on to a night bus to Peshawar could save many nights of walking. Hadn't Chati mentioned seeing the central bus station in Rawalpindi on one of his visits to the dentist? 'You must visit the dentist again,' Dilip told him. 'Find some excuse.'

The idea for a water-carrier came once again from Kamat. They would use the rubber tubing from Coelho's G-suit. An anti-gravity suit is designed to prevent blood from pooling in the lower part of the pilot's body during rapid acceleration. During flight the pilot's G-suit is attached to a valve in the cockpit that automatically fills the tubes with air when necessary. Now Kamat used scissors to carefully remove the tubing from the leg section of Coelho's G-suit. The tube would be filled with water and tied tight before the breakout, then refilled at every opportunity along the way. It would be carried in one of the knapsacks, which had yet to be devised.

Then, one Sunday morning Dilip badly needed the toilet, just when it was occupied. Because Sunday was the camp commander's day off, a guard accompanied him to Wahid-ud-din's office where there was a western toilet. Even on weekdays prisoners with back problems were allowed to use that toilet, and it wasn't Dilip's first time there either. But it was the first time he had taken such careful notice of the long curtains that shaded the window. Though there was just one window it was covered by six strips of coarse cotton cloth, perfect for making knapsacks. He stood on the toilet, took the rod from its holder and removed two of the strips. When he replaced the rod he spread the other strips out. Surely no one will notice the difference, he thought. Then he wrapped the folded strips around his waist, tucked in his shirt, and made his way back to his cell.

The two knapsacks were sewn by Kamat who would have loved to be on the escape team. Since that was out of the question because of his injured legs, he had decided to support the effort in every way possible. All the prisoners had been issued a pair of shorts for the warm weather, traditional army shorts with buckles on either side to adjust the size of the waist. Kamy ripped the buckles from two pairs of shorts and used them as fasteners for the knapsacks. When he finished sewing the knapsacks Dilip hid them under the bedding in Cell 5.

The sewing of the knapsacks and the making of the compass, both time-consuming activities, were risky as well. What if a guard came in to inspect the premises? What if he merely glanced through the bars and said, 'Just a moment. What are you doing in there?' But the guards were enlisted men and the prisoners, all officers. A certain deference was observed. Everyone, guards and prisoners alike, knew the daily routine, and as long as the routine was followed, there were no searching glances, no questions asked, and no cells searched.

To fill all the hours, most of the prisoners had become readers. Some had asked for books early on and Rizvi had obliged. Since then, books from the Chaklala base officers' library—old, tattered copies of the classics, many of them published long before Independence—were placed on the table in Cell 5, picked up and read, then taken back and another batch brought over.

One day Singh found among the batch of fresh books a travel book called *Murray's Handbook, India, Burma and Ceylon*. Popularly known as *Murray's Guide,* the book was first published in 1895. By 1972 it had gone through many editions. The most recent title was *A Handbook for Travellers in India, Pakistan, and Ceylon,* but that was not the edition he discovered.

The copy Singh thumbed through so avidly was obviously published before 1947 but that did not trouble him. It promised 'numerous maps and plans'. Dilip and Grewal were particularly interested in detailed maps of roads and railway lines, and as far as he knew, systems of roads and railways in India and Pakistan hadn't changed in years. If they didn't catch a night bus, the three men could follow the rail line west to Peshawar, hiding during the daylight hours in a culvert under the tracks. The advantages of a rail line were several. First of all, they would know they were going in the right direction. Secondly, they could go for long distances through open country, without encountering the constant traffic of carts, buses and pedestrians they would meet by road. And finally, they could be sure of finding bridges over the rivers they would have to cross. Singh knew that they were particularly concerned about the Indus, which they would be crossing during the monsoon.

Sure enough, *Murray's Handbook* was full of maps and useful descriptions. For major cities there were foldout maps while for less populated areas smaller maps were reproduced on the page showing major geographical features as well as roads, villages and railways. When he turned to the section on the Khyber Pass,

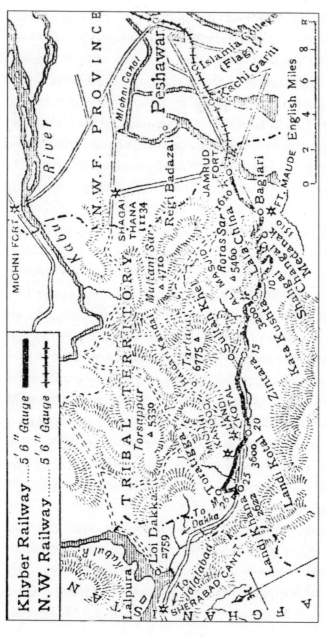

Map of the Khyber Pass taken from *A Handbook for Travellers in India, Burma and Ceylon,*
13th edition, John Murray 1929, p. 388

he was delighted to find that a rail line from Peshawar reached all the way to the Afghan border. Its final stop was a rail station called Landi Khana, directly across from the Afghani town of Torkham. Singh carefully ripped out the pages on the Khyber area and gave them to Dilip.

'No one should leave Peshawar without visiting the Khyber Pass . . . the journey through the pass can now be made by rail from Peshawar.' The guide went on to explain that until the 1920s the railway ended at Jamrud, ten miles west of Peshawar, but in 1925 the Khyber Pass railway was opened, linking Jamrud to the Afghan frontier at Landi Khana. Now a traveller had the choice of going by road or by rail.

The ascent to the Khyber Pass began a little beyond Jamrud but the pass itself was visible from there. The book described the pass as 'exceedingly narrow and hemmed in by cliffs on either side . . . at the summit of the Pass (3509 feet) is the town of Landi Kotal . . . from Landi Kotal a steep descent of 2000 feet leads to Landi Khana, which is 2 miles from the Afghan border.'

Grewal and Dilip imagined themselves walking the ten miles from Peshawar to Jamrud where they would begin the ascent. They might take the road but more likely they would follow the railway line. They both knew the narrow gauge rail line from Kalka to Simla. These old lines climbed gradually. There were no long tunnels or narrow ledges—nothing they couldn't manage. Either way, it looked as though they would have to pass through the town of Landi Kotal, and a few miles further another town with a similar name, Landi Khana.

Dilip hid the page with the map under the blankets on his charpoy. But he hardly needed to look at it again. First to

Peshawar where the Grand Trunk Road ended. Then find the road to Jamrud and from there the rail line to Landi Khana. He couldn't believe his luck. Imagine Singh finding such a valuable book lying on the table!

# Welcome to Khyber
## (13 August)

After walking past the Peshawar airfield, they decided to get off the main road. They set off down another road that branched off to the left and came to a railway line. They presumed this was the rail line from Peshawar to Jamrud they knew about from *Murray's Handbook,* the line they'd thought of following all the way to the Afghan border at Landi Khanna. But when they looked west down the line they could see the outlines of a large village that would be difficult to skirt. They could see people crossing the tracks, some of them women, and they knew in Pakistan the purdah system was taken very seriously. If they tried to cross through a village, or happened to look at a woman, they could attract even more attention, so they decided to head back to Jamrud Road and carry on.

Midway between Peshawar and Jamrud, as they were passing the treed campus of college or university on their right, they noticed some sort of a tollgate or checkpoint on the road ahead. They immediately sought cover in a hedge and debated what to do next. 'We can't go on this way,' said Dilip. 'I think we'd be better off taking a bus.'

And that is what they did. They returned to the road, which at this point was not busy. A little way along the road they found a boy sitting on a parapet and asked about buses. He told them that it was simply a matter of flagging down a bus whenever one came along. Before long a bus appeared and the boy flagged it down. Since the bus was already packed, the boy scrambled up a ladder which was fixed to the rear of the bus and they followed him. The roof already held other passengers and mounds of luggage, but they quickly found space.

Travelling on the roof of the bus seemed to be the norm in this part of the country. Soon another boy mounted the roof to collect the fare. They paid what he asked for the ride as far as Jamrud. At the checkpoint they held their breath as the contents of their bags were examined, but their dried apricots and bag of glucose powder did not interest the inspectors. Even the strange tube of water did not arouse their curiosity. They were looking for grain and nothing else. They would pass another checkpoint and go through the same routine.

Soon they saw Jamrud Gate, a stone arch that spanned the highway. Through the gate they could look straight down the road to a range of mountains, only a few miles ahead. To their right was the famous Jamrud Fort, stretching along the highway like a giant battleship. It had been built by a Sikh general in 1823. Grewal knew that Jamrud Fort had marked the western border of the kingdom of the most powerful of all Sikh rulers, Maharaja Ranjit Singh.

The bus stopped near Jamrud Gate and they shouldered their sacks and climbed down. Strung out along the road near the gate a number of signs were posted, each one warning travellers about proceeding any further.

'You are now entering a tribal area,' read one. 'Visitors are warned not to leave the road,' said another. 'Welcome to Khyber. Visitors are warned not to photograph tribal women.' On and on went the warnings, written in Urdu as well as English. 'Visitors are advised to cross this region during daylight hours,' they read. Of course, apart from photographing tribal women, they intended to break all the rules. Once again, the plan was to leave town, find a place to hide for the rest of the day, and begin their hike through the mountains at night.

The next major town, Landi Kotal, was twenty-five kilometres ahead, uphill most of the way. But they weren't doing badly so far. At this point, it was about eight o'clock in the morning and they had already reached the beginning of the Khyber Pass. Once they attained the summit, at Landi Kotal, it was only another five kilometres downhill to Landi Khanna near the Afghan border.

They set off at a brisk pace and were soon out of town. From Jamrud on all the locals were literally dressed to kill—each one with his gun and ammunition belt. And the countryside was very strange, too. From what they could tell each dwelling, no matter how small, was walled and fortified, like a mini-fortress. The barren plain, dotted with these structures, stretched out around them and a few kilometres ahead were equally barren hills. Scarcely a tree in sight, only some scrubby bush.

Once again, as soon as they set off along the road, they attracted attention from the locals. People walking along the road turned around to stare, and a little boy of about eight, rolling a bicycle tyre along the road, followed them. He took a look at Harry Sinjhi and said, 'Angrezi hai.' (You're English.)

'Angrezi nahin,' responded Harry. 'Pakistani hai.' But the kid didn't give up. After following them for a few minutes longer, he said, 'Pakistani nahin. Hindustani hai.'

At this point Harry chastized the kid for being rude and told him to scram, but all three men felt extremely vulnerable. Perhaps he was simply a naughty kid, throwing insults at strangers he found walking along the road like aliens from another planet. Or could it be that he had watched enough Hindi movies to make a sound judgement? And if an eight-year-old could detect their nationality, what hope did they have? They knew they needed a hiding place immediately.

'A culvert,' said Dilip. 'There is nowhere else. We will have to find a water pipe and scramble in when no one is looking.'

At the next culvert, perhaps a kilometre or two beyond Jamrud, they sat down on the parapet. For a few minutes they were all alone. There was no need to rush. They had already come much farther than they'd ever expected in such a short time. In a minute or two they would head down the embankment and into the culvert and spend the rest of the day there.

Then, in the distance, Dilip spotted a bicycle heading towards them. We will have to wait a little longer he thought. Let this fellow pass. But it turned out the boy had spotted them from afar and had come to meet them. He apparently had no other mission in mind. When he reached them he dismounted, greeted them with 'salaam alaikum', and sat down beside them. A fellow in his late teens, dressed in the typical white salwar kameez of the region, he was very curious and wanted to know all about them. Dilip tried to divert the conversation to the boy himself. He asked him about crops in the area and then about his job. The boy said he had no job, that unemployment was very high. But the diversion didn't work for long. Where were they from, he wanted to know. On the spur of the moment Dilip made up a new story that he hoped would help explain their strange accents and motley appearance.

'We are Pakistanis from overseas,' he said. 'We have come back to see our country.'

The boy seemed to believe him, but the questions continued. When he learned they were hiking to Landi Kotal, he was very concerned. It was much too far to walk, he told them.

'We like to walk,' said Dilip. But before they had a chance to fend him off, their good Samaritan had flagged down a bus and they were once again settling themselves on its roof, as the boy waved them farewell.

Soon they were in the mountains. From the roof of the bus they had a clear view of lookout posts on the peaks, and further down, cave dwellings cut into the slopes, their entrances covered in cloth. At each cave entrance they could see a huge hound standing guard. Whenever the bus passed near one of these dwellings the hound would bark ferociously. Just as well, they realized, that they were not trekking through the territory at night.

# The Simla Conference

In a matter of weeks everything seemed to be falling into place. When Chati returned from his visit to the dentist, he had just the information they needed: 'Turn left on the Mall Road,' he said, 'then left on the first major road after that. You follow that road straight into town. It's a long, long way, likely four or five kilometres, but eventually you will see the central bus station. It's a big field stretching out on your right.'

Finally, on 20 June, the rains began. At first they were neither heavy nor long, just enough to cool the air a few degrees. Then, on 24 June, an ICRC aircraft facilitated the exchange of yet another group of sick and wounded prisoners, and picked up more mail. A day or so later, a Red Cross rep arrived at the camp with another batch of letters and parcels.

Since April, when Wahid had provided a radio, the POWs had enjoyed listening to music and the news for days at a time, though there would also be times when either the radio didn't work or their access to it was removed because the whole camp was put in lockdown mode. These episodes were inevitably touched off by bad news about the Pakistani POWs in India. When that happened Wahid-ud-din would march into Cell 5, often with a newspaper rolled up in his hand, and tell them that a prisoner had been shot.

'Tell me why I shouldn't shoot the lot of you!' he would say, slapping the paper on the table. Then he would stomp out and take the newspaper with him, so they were never sure if he was exaggerating or even making the story up. In any case, it meant no radio, no games, and no meals together. They would spend the rest of the day locked in their cells.

Once they got the radio, the prisoners knew that Wahid-ud-din's stories were true. Some of the 93,000 Pakistani prisoners in India were getting fed up of sleeping in tents, eating a mostly vegetarian diet, and wondering if they'd ever see home again. There were occasional riots and attempted breakouts, shots were fired, and POWs died. Still, the broadcasts by All India Radio from at least some of the camps continued to be aired, and now our friends in Pindi were able to listen for themselves as a Pakistani POW took the microphone, sent greetings to his family and friends and told them not to worry. On one of these broadcasts a fellow mentioned that at his camp they watched Hindi movies weekly.

At the June meeting with the Red Cross rep, the POWs mentioned movies being shown to POWs in India. They were thinking in terms of simultaneous reciprocity, but were aware that showing movies for only ten prisoners was unlikely to happen. The rep had a better idea. 'Why don't you ask for a television set?' he suggested.

They asked Wahid that very day, without much hope of success. To their surprise he promised them that if they were right—if the Pakistani POWs were actually watching movies in their camps—he would have a TV set installed immediately.

As usual, the prisoners' main interest in the visit from the Red Cross was the arrival of mail. In June Dilip received another parcel from his sister. In it were two shirts and one pair of trousers—just the civvies they needed for the escape. He quickly stuffed them back in the Red Cross box and tucked it under his charpoy. For the escape Dilip would wear his green salwar kameez. Grewal would wear the beige terylene shirt over his salwar. As for shoes, they would both have to wear the prison issue cotton running shoes. There was no way around that.

The next day a television set was installed in Wahid-ud-din's office. That evening the volleyball game was cancelled as all ten POWs carried their chairs into the office and sat glued to the tube. Some of them had never watched TV before. They soon discovered that television programming in Pakistan was not nearly as much fun as a good Hindi movie, but the news broadcasts did not disappoint them. They were always hungry for news. And they were delighted to find that the evening news was read by a very beautiful woman called Nilopher Malik. After a few evenings of TV, Dilip and some of the others went back to playing volleyball, but whenever Nilopher Malik came on the air someone called Dilip and he always came running.

Shortly after the prisoners got their TV, President Bhutto arrived in India for peace talks with Prime Minister Indira Gandhi. Before leaving Pakistan Bhutto had declared that the return of POWs and the vacation of occupied territories were at the top of his agenda. (At the time of the ceasefire Indian troops occupied approximately 5000 square miles of Pakistani territory in Sind and Punjab.) However, Indira Gandhi's priorities differed. She wanted a comprehensive settlement of long-standing disputes over Kashmir. A prisoner exchange was not on her agenda at all.

Since the Pakistani Army had surrendered to a coalition of troops representing India and Bangladesh, Sheikh Mujib and his government would have to approve any exchange of prisoners, and that matter was seriously complicated by the war crimes issue. Before the Simla meeting Bangladesh had announced a plan to prosecute over 1000 military POWs. India had agreed to hand over all military prisoners against whom Bangladesh presented 'prima facie' cases. So, even though all 93,000 Pakistani POWs had been escorted out of Bangladesh to the relative safety of camps in India, it was not India alone that controlled their fate. It is difficult to believe that Bhutto did not understand that the whole issue of a prisoner exchange was off the table at Simla. He may have wanted a prisoner exchange more than anything, but it was not going to happen.

All the IAF prisoners knew, of course, came from a few news broadcasts, and Bhutto's statements had raised their expectations. They had no access to the longer commentaries and speculations in newspapers. They were hopeful for the obvious trade-off: peace in Kashmir (where India's position had been disputed by Pakistan since 1947) in return for the prisoner exchange Bhutto said was his top priority. It seemed entirely logical. If it happened, the POWs would benefit in two ways. First they would go home. Second, they might never have to fight another

war. And for Grewal, there would be another bonus. He wouldn't
have to risk his life in an escape attempt. The whole escapade
would have become unnecessary.

Talks between the two leaders began at Simla on 28 June.
Every evening the prisoners filed into Wahid-ud-din's office to
watch the evening news. Nothing was as simple or straightforward
as they had hoped. Pakistan was insisting on getting back
its prisoners and occupied territories before even beginning
to discuss Kashmir. On 1 July, a day before the end of the
conference, Gandhi and Bhutto met briefly but couldn't get past
their stalemate. It seemed the conference was doomed to failure.

By 2 July the prisoners had pretty well given up hope for
the Simla conference. And they had another problem on their
hands. That morning Wahid-ud-din stormed into Cell 5 while
they were still sitting around having breakfast. He slammed
a copy of *The Dawn* on the table. 'Another Pakistani prisoner
shot dead,' he declared. 'You people don't know how to govern!
I could say I shot you since you were all trying to escape.'

His outburst was met by a stunned silence. They'd heard all
this before, but not for a while. Was it possible, they wondered,
that Wahid-ud-din had somehow gotten wind of the escape
preparations? Or was he all steamed up, as usual, because he had
a brother-in-law and a number of friends among the POWs
in India? After his speech he strode out of the room with the
newspaper under his arm, leaving the prisoners to wait for a
lockdown, or even worse—much worse—a search of their cells.
If Cell 5 were searched they would be doomed for sure: the
knapsacks, the rope, the civvies, the maps—there was no way
they could explain them.

But there was no lockdown that day and after a few hours of the normal routine, they realized their fears had been groundless. On the evening of 2 July they watched the TV news, as usual. The Simla conference was still going on. That evening Bhutto and Gandhi were meeting privately in the hope of salvaging five days of negotiations, not to mention weeks of preparation.

On 3 July 1972 Zulfikar Ali Bhutto flew back to Lahore. At the airport he was greeted by thousands of supporters. A tall, handsome man and a charismatic speaker, Bhutto was Pakistan's first civilian leader after fourteen years of military rule. In the controversial 1970 elections, the Pakistan People's Party, which he had founded, won 72 per cent of the votes in West Pakistan. After losing the war and half the country, and all his credibility, President Yahya Khan had been forced to cede power to Bhutto.

That evening the POWs sat in Wahid-ud-din's office watching Bhutto's triumphant return on the evening newscast. It was clear that six months into his presidency, the man was still very popular. He knew just what to say. He talked about losing the war but winning the peace. Give peace a chance, he said. And the people cheered every sentence. At the end of his speech, when he flung his jacket into the crowd, men scrambled for it, tearing it to pieces.

The Simla Agreement, signed very late on the night of 2 July 1972, after intense one-on-one negotiations between the two leaders, did, in fact, become the basis of peace between the two countries for the next forty years. In exchange for the return of 5000 square miles of occupied territory in West Pakistan, Bhutto had agreed to respect the line of control in Kashmir and 'to refrain from threat or use of force in violation of this line'. Indira

Gandhi had achieved her goal. India would continue to govern the majority of Kashmir. Gradually, over the years she expected that the line of control would be recognized as an international border. And as far as India was concerned Gandhi had ceded very little. Retaining the territories in Pakistan that had been occupied as result of the 1971 war had never been her intention.

That evening the prisoners waited to hear something about a prisoner exchange or a reference to negotiations beginning on such an exchange but there was nothing. The next morning Wahid-ud-din came in, his paper tucked under his arm as usual, but this time he was happy, happier than the prisoners had ever seen him. He read them the headline: 'India Returns Territory'. The prisoners asked him to leave the newspaper for them that day and he did. Then, growing bolder, someone said they really should have access to *The Dawn* every day and in his buoyant mood Wahid-ud-din agreed.

Thus the prisoners were able to follow the news closely as the details of the Simla Agreement emerged, but they found nothing encouraging at all. On 12 July Indira Gandhi held her first press conference after signing the pact. When questioned about Indian POWs, she made it clear that there would be no general exchange of prisoners until a firm peace was assured. Since there had been no firm peace between India and Pakistan for twenty-five years, the POWs did not find this news reassuring. It was time to start digging.

Flight Lieutenant A. Vikram Pethia, prisoner of war, being received by his mother and sister, 8 May 1972, Palam

Aditya Vikram Pethia

BHARGAVA
CAPT DUSTOOR
JAFA
TEJWANT SINGH CHATI
KAMAT KURUVILLA
Major Himmat Singh
PAK SECURITY
Major Sher Jaman
PAK SECURITY

Former POWs of the 1971 War on arrival at Lyallpur (now Faisalabad) Jail, end August 1972, watching Janamashthami celeberations by Indian jawans (POWs)

Flight Lieutenant Tejwant Singh presenting an oil painting made by him to the
Chairperson of Pakistan Red Cross

Flight Lieutenant M.S. Grewal meeting his next of kin

Former POWs of the 1971 War arriving for a reception at Ram Bagh by citizens of Amritsar on 1 December 1972

Courtesy of Tejwant Singh

Former POWs of the 1971 War coming out of an AVRO at Palam on
1 December 1972

Former POWs of the 1971 War on arrival at Palam on 1 December 1972

Photo courtesy: Faith Johnston

Malvinder Singh Grewal, February 2013

Photo courtesy: Faith Johnston

Dilip Parulkar, February 2013

The author with Anu and Jawahar Lal Bhargava, February 2013

# The Wall

By the time the digging began, the escape team numbered three. Harish Sinhji's enthusiasm finally overcame Dilip's hesitation to take him along. For weeks Sinhji used all the ammunition he could muster to persuade his comrades that he was a good candidate. Later he confessed, 'I bluffed and said I had come first in the jungle and snow survival course.' But Harry's size and strength wasn't the only issue. The son of a princely family from Mysore, he had always attended English-language schools. Consequently his Hindi was very poor and he spoke no Punjabi at all.

On the other hand, by July the escape had become a group enterprise. The group had decided that only bachelors could go—it was too risky for men with families—and Sinhji qualified on that score. But in the end, it was Harry's persistence that won him a place on the team. He obviously wanted to be part of the escape team so badly that Dilip felt it would be undemocratic not to give him his wish. Yes, he was neither tall nor strong and might slow them down, but he was a fearless fellow and very good-natured. At one point during their sojourn in Pindi Harry received a letter from a woman he had met at a wedding and fallen in love with (as he tended to do). Because the letter was written in Hindi he needed someone to translate it, and that, of course, led to a great deal of teasing, but he had taken it in his usual good form.

Because Harry's Hindi was so atrocious, it was agreed that he would have to keep his mouth shut during the escape. If they were stopped and questioned he would say he was an Anglo-Pakistani from Hyderabad (Pakistan), and a civilian friend of the two PAF airmen. For the escape he would have to wear his beige prison pants and the blue-green shirt from the parcel sent by Dilip's sister. Grewal would wear the other shirt, the beige one, over his salwar. Dilip, of course, would wear the green salwar kurta he'd been wearing every evening.

The next task was to have Sinhji move into the escape room. For three or four nights, Grewal, Chati, Dilip and Harry played bridge after dinner, begging the guards to let Harry linger just a little longer to finish a rubber. Then they suggested that Harry simply move in, and they could play as long as they liked without troubling the guards. Once again the trick worked. It was simple enough for Harish to move his charpoy and few belongings into Cell 5. However, keeping up the pretence of playing bridge night after night wasn't as easy as it sounds. Grewal had no interest or skill in the game at all, and they all had more important matters to think about.

This was the routine. The prisoners in Cell 5 played a sham game of bridge until about ten o'clock. Then they asked a guard to unlock the cell for their nightly trip to the toilet. When all four were once again back in the cell and the guard had turned out the light, Dilip and Grewal, in turn, would begin chipping away at the wall, using the light of a torch. The spot the POWs had chosen was on the back wall a few feet from the corner of the room. They had traced a rectangle in the plaster at ground level, just large enough for a broad-shouldered man to slip through.

In mid-July, as they began chipping the plaster, their chief concern was light. Bhargava had managed to get them a torch by telling a lascar he needed one so that he could read after lights out. As the person doing the chipping lay under the charpoy with the torch in one hand and a chipping instrument in the other, it was essential that no shaft of light escape from the work space. To prevent this Dilip had gathered half a dozen blankets (no one was using blankets in the heat) and draped them over his charpoy so that it was covered on all four sides right to the floor.

Each night, before the work started, they moved Dilip's charpoy out from the wall. Then either Dilip or Grewal lay down on the floor under the charpoy with chipping tools and the torch before the charpoy was shoved back, flush with the wall so that no light could escape. Every half hour or so, the two men changed places.

Their second concern was noise. Although the guards were not curious, or even particularly attentive, they knew if a guard heard something suspicious he could be there in seconds, and the first thing he would do was flip the light switch and catch them red-handed. Thus they could dig only when the guards on duty were at least twenty feet away, or when it was raining. The role of Chati and Sinjhi was to stand near the door and keep an

117

eye on the guards. As an extra precaution, one of them always unscrewed the cell's single light bulb before the work began and replaced it when they had finished.

Of course they realized that if the guard flipped the switch and the light didn't come on, he might investigate (or he might not since power outages were common enough). Their back-up plan was a U-shaped gizmo made of raw wire they called the bazooka. By inserting the ends of the bazooka in the electrical outlet in their room, they could blow the fuse. Perfecting the bazooka had taken some time. When they tested Kamat's first bazooka, there was a small explosion, a spark that made a popping noise, and the bazooka was a charred mess. Now they had a stronger, thicker bazooka to do the job.

The chipping tools they used were better than Dilip's original knife and fork. As well as the screwdriver and scissors they now had a sharp-pointed old engine valve Grewal had bought from a little boy selling cold drinks in the camp. Still it was very hard working from such an awkward position. And it was slow, too. Every time a guard started in their direction, Sinhji or Chati whispered a warning and work stopped immediately. 'Our initial plan was to cut this hole in a week to ten days,' Grewal remembers. 'It ended up taking about fifteen.'

The wall was about 25 centimetres thick. After removing the inner plaster, they had a clear view of the bricks. They were typical bricks of the era, 22.5 x 10 x 10 centimetres. Some were laid lengthwise along the wall. In those sections there was another brick behind them, also laid lengthwise. Next would be a section with two bricks laid side by side pointing outwards. In the end they had to remove only eighteen bricks, but each one was firmly ensconced in mortar that had to be chipped away a bit at a time with as little noise as possible. (Unlike the two prisoners who had blasted their way through a similar wall in one night while Grewal's father was magistrate in Punjab, our prisoners were neither desperate nor reckless, and the presence of four armed guards patrolling through the night was reason enough for caution.) They were amazed at how thick the mortar was and how firmly it held so many decades after construction. By the time they finished the job they had accumulated seven or eight boxes of mortar.

Every night, at about 1.30 a.m., they replaced the loose bricks and stored the debris in an empty Red Cross box (there were always several boxes under beds or in the corner of the room). The next day they would be up by seven, as usual, for breakfast with their mates. The others might occasionally be laggards but since Cell 5 was used for all meals its inmates could never linger in bed. Later in the morning, when the sweeper came through, all ten POWs would avert their eyes from the charpoy in the corner, the one with all the blankets and the spare shoes and plastic slippers lined up along the length of it. They were counting on the sweeper's aversion to touching the footwear of the Indian POWs in the course of his cleaning. And sure enough, they were right. The shoes were always left undisturbed.

Every few days, Bhargava shifted a Red Cross box full of the chipped mortar back to the storage room. So far, everything was going according to plan, but Bhargava was growing more and more worried about his friends. Since they were not inclined to listen to him, he decided to speak to Jafa. He had an argument

that might convince him, as a senior officer, to put a stop to
the whole thing.

The idea that married men couldn't be part of the project
did make some sense, he had to admit. Jafa, Bhargava, Coelho,
Kamat and Singh had wives and children who depended on them
and this crazy scheme could definitely be a widow-maker. Even
young Kuruvilla was married, though the marriage was so recent
that he and his wife had now been apart far longer than together.

But there were people who cared about the single men, too.
That was the point Bhargava used with Jafa. 'Think about their
parents,' he argued. 'You have children. What would you say
if one of your sons were in a prison camp and wanted to break
out? Would you allow it?'

'These men are adults,' said Jafa, 'and they are very brave.
I'm not going to stand in their way.'

Tension mounted as the night of the breakout neared. Dilip
and Grewal knew they could not remove the outer plaster until
the night of the breakout itself. Otherwise, the hole would be
visible from the recruiting compound and petrol pump behind
their cell. Every morning employees at the recruiting office
parked their bicycles near the barbed wire fence which was only
a foot from the wall, so someone was bound to notice.

On the evening of Thursday, 27 July, they dislodged the
final brick. 'Tomorrow night, we go,' said Dilip. But Grewal
wanted to wait. The Simla Pact had just been ratified by both
countries and troop withdrawals were beginning. Again there
were rumours of a prisoner exchange. Why not wait a few more
days to see if they were true?

'I don't want to go back through repatriation,' said Dilip.

'If repatriation is tomorrow I will attempt to escape today. We have wasted enough time already.'

Sinhji took Dilip aside. 'If you force Grewal to go and the whole thing goes wrong, his blood will be on your hands,' he said.

'I'm not forcing anyone,' said Dilip. 'I will go on my own. No one has to come with me.' He meant what he said, but, at the same time, he knew very well that Grewal would never let him go by himself and neither would Sinhji. It was a matter of honour, of keeping one's word. It was a matter of loyalty to a fellow officer.

Then Sinhji suggested they should at least wait another day. The next day (28 July) was a Friday. If they waited until Saturday night, their absence would be discovered on Sunday, which was the camp commandant's day off. Discipline was always slack on Sundays. They might have a few more hours of freedom before the alarm was raised.

'But Dilip was determined,' Sinhji remembers, 'and so we all got ready to go.'

The only uncertainty was the weather. Even during the monsoon there was the occasional clear night with no threat of rain. When that happened, the off-duty staff usually dragged their charpoys outside to catch the breeze. Clear weather meant far too many ears close by to hear the sound of breaking plaster.

But that particular Friday the weather was cooperative and the rain clouds rolled in late in the day as expected. In the evening they ate dinner with their comrades as usual, and wished each other a goodnight. Everyone knew that goodnight really meant goodbye. The others went back to their cells, wondering if they would ever see their three friends again. And what would happen to Chati? He was in danger, too. It is always the initial reaction that is unpredictable and possibly violent. When the guards discovered Chati alone in the cell they were bound to be furious. After all, their jobs would be on the line. They might shoot him in anger or in a calculated move to save their reputations. They could always say they shot him while he was trying to escape.

The plan was to break through the plaster at midnight. Kuruvilla would provide a distraction by calling a guard for a visit to the toilet. The cell he shared with Kamat was on the other side of the yard from Cell 5. He knew the guard would come over and unlock his cell, then wait there to lock him up again after he had made his trip. Thus no guard would be standing close enough to Cell 5 to hear the plaster breaking.

After the required rubber of bridge and lights out, the POWs removed the light bulb and got ready to go. They donned their civvies and concealed their pink prisoner identity cards in the waist bands of their underwear. Should they be caught, they hoped that their identity as prisoners of war would give them some protection. They filled the G-suit tube with water, then packed the two knapsacks with some glucose powder (for energy), dried fruits, first aid kit, rope, and the sections of Chati's old parachute. They each pocketed part of the 180 rupees saved from the common funds.

'We made dummies in our beds,' remembers Sinjhi, 'and covered them with blankets and said goodbye to Chati. We made some sketch maps showing we were heading south to Sind, crumpled them up and threw them in the corner of the room to mislead the inevitable search party.'

By this time the rain had started. Their timing, it seemed, was perfect. The guards on duty sought shelter, and those off duty were sound asleep inside the barracks. Kuruvilla had called a guard for the toilet and that guard was probably cursing his luck as he stood over there in the rain waiting for him to return.

Grewal got down to break the outer layer of plaster. First he gave it a push with his hand, but it didn't give. It was stronger stuff than he'd reckoned on. When a simple push didn't work, he pounded it with the heel of his hand, then kicked it with his foot. After a pause, he asked someone to hand him the cricket bat. He tied a rubber sandal to the bat and used it as a battering ram.

'He banged and banged,' Sinhji remembers, and he was finally able to make a small hole the size of a fist. What they had thought was a thin layer of plaster turned out to be much thicker and stronger than they had expected.

By this time one of the guards had heard the noise and rushed to flip the switch outside the cell door. When the light didn't come on the first time, the guard flipped the switch again and again.

'What's going on?' yelled Dilip.

'The light's out,' said the guard.

'Is that you Shams-ud-din?' responded Dilip, as he banged the light bulb in the palm of his hand to break the filament. 'Don't worry about the light. It's always going out. We'll see about it tomorrow. Don't stand there in the rain.'

After a few more clicks of the switch Shams-ud-din left. Seconds later, the bulb was in its socket and everyone was in bed. They expected Shams-ud-din to return with the keys and check the light himself. To their surprise, he never came back. The next morning the POWs were prompt to complain about the burnt out light bulb in their cell. How were they going to play bridge if they couldn't see?

A few days later, they resumed their work on the wall. Before making another attempt, they would have to weaken the plaster by scraping a trough along its periphery. As for the fist-sized hole Grewal had made with the cricket bat, they stuffed it with a dirty piece of cloth so no light would show, and kept their fingers crossed that no one on the outside would notice it. But one night, while Dilip was under the bed, scraping away, he saw the cloth move. Someone on the other side of the wall had to be poking at it. He immediately grabbed the cloth to keep it in place, but could feel someone pulling it in the other direction. The tug of war went on for several seconds, long enough for all four men to be sure the jig was up. Then Dilip lost the battle and the cloth disappeared entirely. When he put his eye to the hole, he was able to glimpse his opponent. 'It's the damned cat,' he whispered.

The new chipping operation was finished in less than a week. Then it was a matter of watching the weather. Several times they watched the clouds gather before sunset, and bid their comrades goodbye after dinner, but at ten o'clock, as they stepped out of the cell to go to the toilet, the sky was as clear as a bell.

'There were at least three occasions,' Bhargava remembers, 'when we had said goodbye and good luck to our heroes and then retired for the night, and to our surprise we saw them in the same room next morning.'

And so arrived the weekend of 12–14 August 1972. On

Monday, 14 August, Pakistan would celebrate its twenty-fifth year of independence from Britain (India would celebrate the same anniversary the following day). There was certainly less for Pakistan to celebrate in 1972 than there had been in 1971. Half the country had chosen to secede, and thousands of Pakistani prisons of war awaited repatriation. Nevertheless, it was a holiday weekend and Camp Commandant Wahid-ud-din would spend it with his family in the hill station of Murree. The cat was away . . .

'The camp commandant was on a trip to Murree,' says Sinhji. 'The Warrant Officer in charge, Rizvi, lived at the other end of town. The camp was in the hands of a dim but lovable corporal called Mehfooz Khan . . . During the early evening stroll, Jafa spotted a flash of lightening and told Dilip a storm was building up. "Go around midnight or earlier if the storm hits before that," he advised.'

This time only Kamat and Kuruvilla, who shared a cell, were actually told of the impending attempt, though others may have suspected. It was, once again, Kuruvilla's task to call for a guard around midnight and say he needed the toilet.

As usual, the POWs in Cell 5 went through their routine of bridge, toilet, and lights out. For the third time, Sinhji, Dilip and Grewal changed into civvies, and filled the knapsacks. They would leave it to Chati to arrange the dummies in their beds. Then Grewal lay down under the charpoy to break the plaster. The plan was for each man to stand close to the outside wall until the next fellow, on a signal from Chati, reached through the hole and tapped his leg to say the coast was clear. Then he would scoot across the alley between the two buildings. Grewal, the first out, waited for a leg tap from Sinhji, who waited for a leg tap from Dilip..

This time the plan worked. The plaster broke. Each man crawled out, waited by the wall, then dashed across the narrow alleyway. It was around midnight. The storm hadn't broken, but a fierce wind fired dust and sand onto their faces. As for the watchman in the adjoining compound, there he was, sitting on his charpoy, perilously close. But when they took a closer look at him, they realized he had put a blanket over his head!

# Landi Kotal

The bus wound up one mountain after the other, then came to a broad gorge with steep walls on either side. There were no more cave dwellings, just craggy walls of shale and limestone closing in on them. After a few more miles the walls of rock retreated and they could see ahead a broad valley or plateau ringed with mountains. Soon the bus pulled into Landi Kotal, the town at the summit of the Khyber Pass. It was a little before ten o'clock but Landi Kotal was already teeming with people. Sunday, it turned out, was market day.

After getting off the bus, the trio again sought the shelter of a dhaba for tea. All they had to do was find the road to Landi Khana and be off. Ten hours on the road and only a few miles to go!

Had they known what was happening back at the camp, they might have had even more confidence in their success. Chati had done a good job of cleaning up the rubble, replacing the bricks, and making sure the blankets folded on the beds resembled his roommates. The next morning he made excuses for them.

'We played bridge too late last night,' he said. 'They're still sleeping.'

When breakfast was ready, rather than rouse the three sleepers so that the POWs could have breakfast together in Cell 5 as usual, the attendants set out breakfast in the former interrogation room. If the camp commandant or even MWO Rizvi had been on duty, it would have been a different story.

Meanwhile, in Landi Kotal, the three men once again played the role of tourists. 'While drinking tea,' says Sinjhi, 'we casually asked the locals where this place called Landi Khana was. They did not seem to know so they asked their neighbours in a sort of "pass it on" game. About the fifth or sixth chap seemed to have some idea and he pointed to one road and said it was about four miles that way.'

'Any buses to Landi Khana?' asked Grewal, who was still doing the talking. The fellow told him that there were no buses, but he could get a taxi for thirty rupees. Thinking that being too generous with their money had aroused the tongawala's suspicions in Peshawar, Grewal decided to reject the price.

'Thirty rupees for four miles!' Grewal exclaimed. 'That's too much! We'll walk.'

With this, they left the dhaba and headed to the bazaar where they'd been told cotton caps were for sale. Everyone else was wearing them, and Dilip figured their lack of caps was what had been attracting much of the attention.

'No cap for me,' said Harry. 'An Anglo-Pakistani would never wear a cap.'

Of course neither would any Christian, but at this point Dilip was not considering their assumed identities. No one had asked their names so far, and he was sure it was their appearance that was out of sync. So he left the two others standing by the road, and went down to the market, which was not far from the dhaba where they'd had tea. When he returned he had two caps, but neither fit Grewal's large head, so he donned his own and dove once more into the market to buy a larger cap.

And that was the mistake that he would forever regret. If only he had not returned to the market the second time. If only he had forgotten about the caps altogether. If only they had taken that first offer of a taxi for thirty rupees. They could have been on the road in minutes. They could have been halfway to Landi Khana by the time he returned with the second cap. But they hadn't taken the first taxi, and by the time he returned from his second trip to the cap-seller, the game was almost up.

# The Tehsildar

When Dilip returned from his second trip to the market, he found Grewal and Sinhji besieged by taxi drivers. First a boy from the tea shop had shouted to them that a driver would take them to Landi Khana for twenty-five rupees. No, said Grewal. It would not do, he thought, for such a scruffy-looking group to spend freely. It would attract attention. Then he had second thoughts. Perhaps they *should* take a taxi. It would be so simple. They could be there in minutes. Sinjhi agreed. As soon as Dilip returned they would make their decision. But before that could happen they were surrounded by taxi drivers, all wanting to take them to Landi Khana.

Dilip returned in the midst of the hubbub. Yes, he said, a taxi is a good idea, and the sooner the better. Attracting a crowd like this was the last thing they needed.

'You want to go to Landi Khana?' said a measured voice from the crowd.

They turned and saw a middle-aged man with a beard who

wore glasses. Another taxi driver, they thought.

'Yes, that's where we're going,' Grewal answered.

Then, instead of joining the other drivers in the bidding war, the new fellow began to question them. At first he was polite. 'Who are you?' he asked them in Urdu. 'Where do you come from?' Grewal told the prepared story about two airmen on vacation, with a civilian friend along.

'How do you know about this place called Landi Khana?' the fellow asked next. 'Do you know someone there?'

Grewal explained that they were exploring the area and had heard Landi Khana was a pretty place to visit. 'It's on all the maps,' he said. It's the terminus of the bloody railway, he was thinking. Surely it has to be a good-sized town.

'No,' said the chap. 'You won't find Landi Khana on any map. Most people have never even heard of the place. It's been abandoned ever since the British left.'

The man then accused them of being Bengalis attempting to escape over the border to Afghanistan. Until this point, our trio did not realize that hundreds of Bengalis had escaped by the same route they were taking. When the war had broken out the 4,00,000 Bengalis living in West Pakistan were unable to leave. And even months after the war, the situation had not improved. Many had been put under house arrest or in camps. They had become another bargaining chip in the peace negotiations between India and Pakistan and Bangladesh. In fact, they were such a valuable commodity that Bhutto had offered a bounty of a thousand rupees for any Bengali caught trying to escape.

Despite the bounty, a number of Bengalis had been successful. Some of them had connections. Some had lived in West Pakistan for years and knew enough to hire smugglers to take them over the border at night. They had savings and jewellery to help finance the operation. But a few of them, it seems, were less knowledgeable or more desperate and, according to the man with the glasses, some had been caught right here in Landi Kotal.

'Do we look like Bengalis?' said Grewal, laughing, as he appealed to the crowd, which was growing by the minute.

But no one else was in a mood to laugh. The man with the glasses seemed to have authority. Only the taxi drivers continued their clamour. As far as they were concerned the inquisitive man was interfering with business. They continued to push in, grabbing the trio's hands and arms in an effort to take them towards their taxis.

But the man with the glasses prevailed. He told our three tourists to show him the contents of their knapsacks and they obeyed. Nothing suspicious in there, they thought, nothing that couldn't be explained. But as soon as he saw a length of Chati's blood-stained parachute, the man looked worried. 'Perhaps he thinks we have killed someone,' Sinhji remembers thinking.

Next the man asked for some identification papers and their PAF leave certificates. Too risky, they said, to carry such important documents with them, but the man was not convinced. He insisted on marching the three men under armed escort (and there was no shortage of armed escort in Landi Kotal) to the office of the tehsildar.

The term, tehsildar, an office that existed since Mughal times, is still in use in both India and Pakistan. The trio realized that they were about to be questioned by the area's top administrative officer. Only the district political agent had more authority. And they soon learned that the man with the glasses was the tehsildar's clerk. No wonder he had known the history of Landi Khana. Everything to do with land, and collecting taxes on land and crops, passed through the tehsildar's office.

The tehsildar, a large man dressed in a salwar kurta, did not budge when they were brought into his office. He sat behind a long table, leaned back in his chair, and began to question them along the same lines as the previous inquisition by his clerk. Who were they? Why were they not carrying any form of identification?

'At the end of an hour in which we'd invented fathers' names and home addresses, (the tehsildar) said that although he could not put a finger on it, he knew there was something very fishy. So fishy, he declared, that he was putting us in jail,' remembers Sinhji. They would remain in jail, the tehsildar told them, until he could determine if the identities they had claimed were true. It might take as long as ten days.

The adventure was over and they all knew it. And being returned to the camp at Rawalpindi was the least of their worries. They all knew they would be lucky to survive ten days in a local prison. Once their true identities were discovered, they would be beaten, possibly shot. If the local population hated Bengalis, they could imagine their feelings towards Indian pilots who had bombed their country only eight months before. And they doubted very much that the tehsildar knew anything about the Geneva Conventions. Even if he did, the matter would soon be out of his hands. They would be at the mercy of the guards at the local prison. All three men had memories of being beaten by locals the previous December, and this time, surrounded by men

# The Escape Route

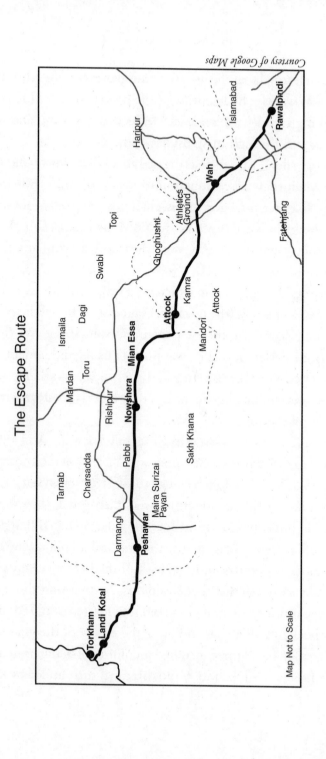

Courtesy of Google Maps

Map Not to Scale

armed to the teeth, they knew their fate was bound to be worse.

Their blood will be on my hands, thought Dilip with horror. Sinhji had been right all along. Dilip was their leader. If not for his insistence, Grewal and Sinhji would not be in this mess. They had been the cautious ones. He had been so hell-bent on escape that he'd never had a second thought. Not until now. And now, here they were in a serious jam and if they all came to a sticky end, he knew it would all be his fault. It was up to him to do something, but what could he say that hadn't already been said?

At this point he noticed a phone on the tehsildar's table and had an idea. It came to him in a flash. Their captor was not the highest-ranking official. Dilip knew that the armed forces in Pakistan commanded even more authority than they did in India. If he could reach their first camp commandant, Usman Hamid, he could put the matter directly in his hands. Usman Hamid was a reasonable man. And as ADC to the PAF chief, he had some clout. If only Dilip could reach Usman Hamid, the tehsildar would have no jurisdiction. He would have to do as directed.

'You can check our identities right now,' he told the tehsildar. 'All you have to do is let me phone Air Force Headquarters.'

The tehsildar was reluctant at first, but Dilip did not give up. 'We fought for this country,' he said with indignation, 'and this is the way you treat us? You want to put us in jail and you won't even let me make a phone call?'

Eventually the tehsildar booked a call to Air Force Headquarters in Peshawar. A few minutes later, when the call went through, he handed the phone to Dilip who asked to speak to the ADC to the Chief of Air Staff.

With the greatest of luck, Squadron Leader Usman Hamid picked up the phone, wondering who could be calling him from Landi Kotal.

'Salaam alaikum, Sir,' said Dilip. 'This is Corporal Phillip Peters, Sir, Phillip, Sir, you know Dilip, from Pindi, Sir. Three of us took some leave to go hiking. These people have caught us.'

The astonished Usman said, 'Dilip, is that you?'

'Yes, Sir.'

'What are you doing in Landi Kotal?'

'We were just trekking up to Torkham, Sir. We told the tehsildar that we are airmen from Lahore, but he is insisting on ID. Sir, please tell him that you know us so he will let us go.'

'Good lord,' said Hamid. 'Let me speak to the tehsildar.'

After a brief conversation the tehsildar put the phone down with great satisfaction. 'I was right,' he told them. 'You may be Pakistani airmen, but you are wanted men. I'm to hold you here until the Air Force police arrive.'

The tehsildar ordered his clerk to take the prisoners to the town jail, and they set off, accompanied once again by an entourage of armed men. Our trio was feeling somewhat relieved not to be facing a week or more in the Landi Kotal lock-up, though they didn't want to show it. Dilip was amazed that his idea had actually worked, and optimistic that somehow Usman would get them out of this mess. Soon, perhaps before the end of the day, they would be whisked away from Landi Kotal in the hands of a police force they could trust to deliver them, intact, back to their camp in Rawalpindi. They might not have to spend a night in the local jail after all.

It was a long walk to the jail on the other side of town. When they arrived they entered a small one-storey building that was unbelievably filthy and buzzing with flies. 'There was excrement in the cells, cobwebs, terrible smells,' remembers Dilip. 'We wouldn't have lasted a week in that place.'

Before locking them up, their jailers told them they must do a body search. That was the rule ('kanoon'). In the course of the search the POW identity cards fell out of their waist bands. The policemen studied the cards. They obviously recognized the photos but couldn't read the English. One of them took the cards and left the building.

'We wondered what would happen next,' writes Sinhji. 'We didn't have long to wait though. The tehsildar, whose name was Shah Tehan, arrived with a posse of tall grim-looking locals. He asked us our names again. This time we gave our real identities for we saw him holding our identity cards. He was so furious that he was shaking with rage.'

'Why did you lie?' he shouted. 'Kaffirs! POWs! How many escaped? From where?'

The tirade went on and on. Dilip was thankful that they were already locked in the filthy cell. At least the tehsildar was doing his rant on the other side of the bars. But their prospects were now as dismal as they had been back in the office. 'It looked like a firing squad for us in the next few minutes,' Sinhji remembers thinking.

After a few minutes a messenger came running in and whispered something in the tehsildar's ear. His tirade against the POWs ended abruptly. He gave some orders in Pashto. Keys and handcuffs were produced. 'Here we go,' they thought.

The trio was handcuffed and chained to one another and

marched back through town, accompanied by the tehsildar and his armed locals. It was another long march. Part way, they passed the tehsildar's office, but they didn't stop there. On they walked, sure they were being led to face a firing squad. Finally the tehsildar told them, 'The political agent wants to see you.'

When they reached his office, the political agent, Mr Burki, came out to meet them. A youthful, clean-shaven man, smartly dressed in Western clothes, Burki exuded authority. As the tehsildar stood gaping, Burki ordered the prisoners' chains and handcuffs removed. Then he shook hands with each one of them. 'Congratulations on a fine attempt,' he said. 'Hardly anyone gets caught in Landi Kotal. The border is four miles down the road—just one hill to cross. You really had bad luck running into the tehsildar's clerk.'

'How about giving us another twenty minutes?' joked Dilip. 'That way we can keep the record clean.'

Once they entered the building they were taken to a hall of honour, the Jirga room, where tribal chiefs held their meetings. Burki gave instructions to his staff that the prisoners were to be treated with the same respect and decorum as visiting Pakistani officers. 'They are our guests,' he said. *'Dumba qatal kar.'* (Kill the lamb.)

Soon armchairs and a table were brought to the dais, and a wonderful feast was laid out for them. There was rice, lamb, melons, and other savoury dishes. They realized how hungry they were. They were almost certain they had Usman, as well as Burki, to thank. Surely it was Usman who had informed the political agent of their presence in Landi Kotal. If it weren't for

Usman, they would still be dealing with the furious tehsildar and his rough cohorts.

After the feast they waited an hour or two for the arrival of the PAF police. But that time passed quickly. They were all so exhausted they dozed in their chairs.

Meanwhile, back in Rawalpindi, all the prisoners knew that the escape had taken place even before they sat down to breakfast. On his way to the toilet Singh noticed Chati sitting in Jafa's cell. 'The sparrow has flown,' Chati whispered to Singh. Thus the word passed, as each man made his way to the toilet, which was next to Jafa's cell. 'The sparrow has flown,' was whispered again and again. Once they sat down to a late breakfast in the interrogation room, tension was high. How long would the guards let three prisoners 'sleep on' before they investigated?

Since no one wanted to be alone when the escape was discovered, after breakfast most of the men sought company. Only Coelho remained alone in Cell 2. Chati returned to Jafa's cell, where he had taken shelter earlier that morning, so that he could let his colleagues sleep on. Kuruvilla and Kamat were together in the cell they shared. Singh retreated to Bhargava's cell, which was directly across the courtyard from the escape cell. For over an hour Singh and Bhargava played cards, but their minds were not on the game.

'We were all the time waiting to face the storm that would break out any time,' Singh remembers. 'We discussed all kinds of possibilities, including being lined up and shot . . . We were aware of Pakistani POWs having been shot dead when they tried to break out of camps in India.'

But the calm continued. What could be happening, they

wondered? By ten o'clock, the escape still hadn't been discovered. The two men continued to play cards, their eyes wandering frequently to the door of the cell across the yard.

Eventually the action was set off by a phone call taken in the guardroom by the corporal on duty. Singh and Bhargava didn't hear the phone, but they did see the corporal hurry across the courtyard to the residence of the PAF staff. In a few minutes he returned to the guardroom with a flight sergeant.

At this point, around ten thirty or so, a commotion erupted in the camp. 'It was real hulchul,' Bhargava remembers. 'Guards ran helter-skelter and we knew the news was out. One guard started counting us and soon we saw guards opening the escape room and removing the beds.'

Soon all seven POWs were separated and locked in solitary cells with both doors locked. Singh remembers being taken from Bhargava's cell to his own on the other side of the courtyard. It was a distance of twenty to twenty-five metres. The guards, with whom he'd spent months establishing an amicable relationship, were angry and on edge. They kept him in their gun sights the whole way. It had been like that in the beginning, and now tension was high all over again.

All the cells were searched and everything was taken away. They lost slippers and books and letters from home. Each man was left with the clothes he was wearing and his toothbrush. Singh was glad that he had hidden his roll of notes in the toilet. It was a miracle that the notes—a diary that he had been writing for months—had not been concealed in his shoe when the first search took place. He used to write notes in his cell then transport them to the toilet in his shoe. He had found a crevice in the flush tank's support system (the whole thing was loose) and that was his usual hiding place. Should the notes be discovered, no one would know where they came from. If they were discovered in his cell or on his person, he might be in trouble.

'I am sure that each of us in the camp went through the same,' says Bhargava. The worst thing for most of them was the sudden and complete rupture in their relationships with the staff. 'MWO Rizvi visited my cell and said, "Enemy will remain as enemy. We trusted you all and look what you have given us in return."'

And Bhargava knew that Rizvi had a point. Most of them had considered Rizvi a friend. The escape had broken the trust and goodwill they had nurtured with him and other guards and attendants at the camp. The staff at the camp would be held responsible. What would happen to Rizvi, to the compliant Aurangzeb, to Shams-ud-din and Mehfooz Khan and all the other staff?

But, at that moment, Bhargava didn't dwell on their fate. He was more interested in the fate of his three brothers, who, as far as he knew, were still out there somewhere, trudging west to the Khyber Pass. Now that the escape had been discovered, the heat was on.

# Aftermath

At about four o'clock in the afternoon, three jeeps, each one carrying three members of the PAF police, pulled up to the office of political agent Burki in Landi Kotal. The policemen were a rough and angry lot. Each prisoner was handcuffed and his ankles were shackled. Dilip was pushed into the back seat where he sat between two guards, his shackles anchored to the floor. In the front seat, another armed guard sat beside the driver. Before taking off, each prisoner was blindfolded. The ride to Peshawar took less than an hour, but they were not told where they were being taken, so tension was still high.

At the Peshawar air base, the jeeps pulled up in front of an old prison. The blindfolds and shackles were removed and the men were led down a long corridor to their cells. In fact, there were only two cells available, so Dilip, as senior officer, was housed in a converted office, much larger than a cell. On one wall was a fireplace with an iron grill. In the centre of the room sat a large rectangular table. At one time, years before, there had obviously been a stove in the centre of the room, where the table was now. When Dilip looked at the ceiling near the fan, he could see that most of the chimney hole had been filled in but there was still a small gap. He thought it might be possible to knock out some mortar and escape through the old chimney hole.

'I was completely obsessed with the idea of escape,' he admits now. 'I could think of nothing else. It was all amateurish and a very silly thing to do.'

His first step was to pry loose one of the iron bars from the grill of the fireplace. Then he placed a chair on the table, so that he could reach the high ceiling, and began to poke away at the mortar in the old chimney hole. As he was standing on the chair he heard keys jangling outside the office door. The guard had a set of keys and was trying one after another. By the time he found the right key and opened the door, Dilip had the chair off the table, and the iron bar back in its place.

As soon as the guard locked the door, Dilip mounted the table again. This ritual was repeated several times. Each time, as soon as he heard the keys jangle, he quickly got down. By the third or fourth time, the guard had become faster at finding the correct key, and caught him in the act of removing the chair from the table.

'I was trying to adjust the fan,' Dilip explained.

'The regulator is over there,' said the guard, pointing to the wall by the door.

But the guard was not fooled. Before long, he returned to shift Dilip to Grewal's cell, and Grewal to the converted office. Now Dilip was in a more secure room, but still, to make absolutely sure he would not make another attempt, the guard handcuffed him to a bar of the cell door and left the light on.

Dilip decided to raise a great fuss. 'Get the provost marshal here,' he shouted. 'I'm an Indian officer and won't accept this treatment!' He kept shouting until the guard turned off the light in his cell. That hardly made a difference because the section of the cell nearest the doorway was flooded with light from the corridor. Nevertheless, despite the heat, the mosquitoes, and the light, he slid his handcuff down the bar so that he could lie on a blanket (there was no bed in the cell) and sleep for the first time in two nights.

When breakfast arrived the next morning, he declared he was on a hunger strike. 'I'm an Indian officer,' he said, with indignation. 'I should not be treated in this manner. Until I see the provost marshal, I will not eat.'

Before long the base commander arrived and ordered Dilip's handcuff removed. He also agreed that Dilip and Sinhji, both housed in regular cells, would be provided with table fans. 'If you behave yourself we will be nice to you,' he said, 'but if you misbehave we know how to handle you.'

'Okay,' said Dilip. 'I will not do anything. Could I please have my breakfast now?'

When they heard this his friends down the corridor had to laugh. 'Must be the shortest hunger strike in history!' shouted Grewal.

'Well it got results!' countered Dilip

They stayed in Peshawar several nights. Since the fans were carefully placed outside the grill of the two cells, and the corridor light was always on, there was really little relief from either heat or light, and the mosquitoes continued to buzz and bite. On

15 August, Indian Independence Day, some Pathans among their guards furtively brought them a delicious chicken dish and some grapes. Otherwise, their sojourn in Peshawar was hot and humiliating. But Dilip had anticipated much worse. 'I expected to be tortured day in and day out,' he remembers, 'so everything was a bonus.'

On the fourth or fifth day after their initial escape, the three men were once again handcuffed, shackled and blindfolded, and loaded into two vehicles. Again they were not told where they were going. Soon they were out of town, on a highway, going God knows where. When they pulled over, Dilip wondered if they were going to be lined up and shot. Despite his confidence in Usman, he couldn't get the idea out of his mind. He had read in a Western comic that you never hear the shot that kills you. But the stop was simply a bathroom break and a halt for tea. After a few more hours on the road, they drove through the gates of No. 3 Provost and Security Flight in Rawalpindi and their blindfolds were removed.

There they were, back in that old, familiar place, but they recognized no one. Their comrades had disappeared and the whole staff had changed. 'Where has everyone gone?' asked Dilip.

'We have shot them all,' said a sergeant. Surely he was joking! But it was hard to be sure of that.

In fact, while the three escapees were being held in Peshawar, their comrades spent three very uncomfortable days and nights in solitary confinement. Instead of the usual friendly conversation, they were cursed by their guards and kept in gun sights whenever they crossed the courtyard to go to the toilet.

At night they were wakened almost hourly for body searches. Chati was questioned twice in the interrogation room. He stuck to his story: he had known nothing of the escape plans. His roommates had fooled him as well as everyone else.

On the third night, the seven prisoners were awakened before dawn and breakfast was delivered to their cells shortly afterwards. They were told to prepare for a trip. There was little to prepare, though they did receive some of their possessions back. Night clothes and toiletries, Jafa's notebook, Coelho's dictionary, these things were returned helter-skelter and quickly bundled up for the trip. One by one they made their trips to the toilet. When it was Singh's turn, he reached into the crevice where he had hidden his notes and found them gone. Possibly someone had given the chain a great yank and the notes had tumbled into the latrine and gone down the drain, unobserved. However it had happened, months of work had disappeared and he now had no notes to jog his memory.

Early that morning, the seven prisoners were assembled in the courtyard where several jeeps stood waiting. There was the camp commandant, Wahid-ud-din, hands on hips, directing the operations. His anger was obvious. They were bloody scoundrels, he told them. He had given them all sorts of privileges. He had trusted them and they had let him down. 'Now,' he said, 'you will be taken to a place where you will never see the daylight.'

After Wahid-ud-din's harangue, the POWs were blindfolded and handcuffed and seated in the jeeps where the chains on their cuffs were fastened to the belt of a guard seated beside them. The jeeps drove out the gate and turned right. Seven blindfolded pilots took note of the turns, the traffic noises, the angle of the sun on their faces. They were going south. In the small gap between blindfold and cheek, some could see the floor of the jeep and if their heads jerked back (it was a bumpy road) they could make out the occasional road sign, always in Urdu. Singh was one of these. Putting together all the clues, before long he guessed they were heading towards Lahore.

After about two hours the jeeps turned off the main road onto a rougher road, and a few minutes later they pulled off that road and started into a field. This was an alarming development. 'Looking at the scene through the gap, I began to wonder if we were going to be taken to some remote area to be disposed of,' remembers Singh. He knew the story of *The Great Escape*—over seventy prisoners escaped initially, probably the largest POW escape in history, but only three made it to safety. Fifty of those who had been recaptured were taken into a forest and shot.

Soon the jeeps stopped. Their blindfolds and handcuffs were removed. Wahid-ud-din shouted to some locals, who were peering around a building, to bring charpoys. Once the prisoners were seated, tiffin tins were unloaded and they ate lunch. Wahid-ud-din's bark was definitely worse than his bite.

After lunch, their journey started again, complete with blindfolds and handcuffs, and after a few more hours, those who could glimpse the outside world spied the massive walls and gate of a prison. The jeeps stopped outside the gate. Wahid-ud-din left his charges and entered the compound. After a few minutes, the POWs were escorted inside and their blindfolds and handcuffs removed. They found themselves standing in the open air but everywhere they looked were walls. The outer walls of the prison were at least fifteen feet high and topped with several layers of barbed wire. And inside the high outer walls were a series of other compounds with walls at least eight feet high. It was a far cry from No. 3 Provost and Security Flight in Rawalpindi. The whole place looked newly built and built to last.

'Welcome to Lyallpur,' said the man standing before them. He was a clean-shaven man of average height and girth, in his forties or early fifties, they guessed. 'I'm in charge here. My name is Lieutenant Colonel Latif.'

'Now I know you are duty-bound to try and escape,' he went on, 'but it is my duty to stop you. And I must warn you, that wire you see up there is electrically charged. As you know, your friends have been caught, and they will join you here soon.'

They heard this news with great relief. Until then they had heard rumours, but this was the first official word of their comrades' safety. They liked Latif immediately. They liked his humour, his frankness and his courtesy, all in such contrast to the way Wahid-ud-din had been treating them. He invited them to take tea in the office compound nearby. Over tea—served in china cups, not the usual enamelled mugs they'd become used to—he told them that he had a particular sympathy for POWs because his own brother was a POW in India. He also told them that the office compound, where they were having tea, was earlier the lock-up for Sheikh Mujibur Rahman (now president of Bangladesh). When they finished their tea, he took them to see a garden the Sheikh had planted to while away his time.

Wahid-ud-din did not linger to see the garden. He left immediately after tea without saying a word to the prisoners. He had a long road ahead of him. Back to Rawalpindi he would go and face the real culprits. Once the inquiry was finished he could wash his hands of the whole lot of them.

After their arrival at No. 3 Provost and Security Flight, the notorious three were taken to cells 1, 2 and 3, nearest the guardhouse, to await their trial. As he crossed the courtyard from the jeep to his cell, Grewal muttered to his escort, 'I tried to be an honourable man, and here I am in handcuffs.'

'Not handcuffs,' said the man. 'Those are your jewels.'

It was a remark he would never forget and it helped him get through the difficult days ahead. They were in solitary confinement once again, eating meals in their cells. Their only contacts were guards who were not as sympathetic as Grewal's initial escort. In fact, most of them were actively hostile.

'You'd better not try anything funny,' one fellow warned Dilip. 'We are all sharpshooters and judo black belts. If you try anything funny, I'll break every bone in your body and shoot you dead.'

'Well, no one saw me go the first time,' he replied coolly, 'and no one will see me go this time either.' Somehow he was still riding high, and the threats only fuelled his adrenaline.

For two days the Chaklala base commander conducted a court of inquiry into the escape. Each man was interviewed separately on two occasions and then brought in again for sentencing. The court took place in Wahid-ud-din's office, where they had watched TV in the evenings. The procedure was familiar to all three men. It was the same as a court of inquiry into some mishap or misdemeanour in the Indian Air Force. The president of the court, in this case the base commander from Chaklala, asked the questions, and another officer took notes.

At the end of the process, Wahid-ud-din, as camp commander, sentenced each man to thirty days solitary confinement, the maximum penalty allowed under the Geneva Conventions. When the prisoners asked for the days they had already spent in solitary confinement in Peshawar and Pindi to be counted towards those days, Wahid agreed.

'He had to be nice to us,' reflects Grewal. 'His fate was in our hands.' Later, after they emerged from solitary confinement and were finally able to compare notes, the trio discovered that they had all come, independently, to the same decision not to cast aspersions against the staff at the camp or complain about the conditions.

'We had tricked people,' says Dilip. 'They had cooperated involuntarily and we didn't want to get them into trouble.' Therefore he was careful not to mention the compass (still in his shirt pocket) or the batteries used to magnetize it, or the map from *Murray's Handbook*, which had come on loan from the Chaklala base library. As to their motives for the escape, he said poor treatment or good treatment had nothing to do with it. They were prisoners of war and it was simply their duty to escape if at all possible.

After sentencing, they were once again blindfolded, handcuffed and shackled, and taken to the railway station where they boarded a night train. The security was even more impressive than before. Each prisoner occupied his own air-conditioned compartment, his handcuffs chained to either a bar of the window or a bunk support. In the same compartment, an armed guard kept constant watch. A sergeant who escorted Dilip to the toilet consented to unlocking the handcuffs, but he was clearly nervous. After a short interval he banged on the toilet door and said, 'Sahib, what are you scheming now?'

Early in the morning, the trio were blindfolded and taken off the train into vehicles. When the blindfolds were removed, they, too, were welcomed to Lyallpur by Lt Col Latif who once again gave his spiel on their duty to escape and his duty to stop them, and pointed out the electrical wire that topped the outer walls. Then he led them into his office where he examined their documents. Sensing Latif's good nature, Grewal decided it was worth asking him to excuse them from the rest of their term in solitary.

'The army is a much larger and more generous organization than the air force,' Grewal said, hoping the man would respond to flattery, but Latif only laughed.

They were put in high-security cells. Each cell had access to a walled courtyard about two metres square that had a wire roof. The sun managed to penetrate this enclosure for just a few hours each day. The rest of the cell was cramped. There was a cement plinth for sleeping, a squat toilet and a tap. On the cement plinth was a thin mattress. The chain for the toilet was located outside each cell, which meant calling the guard for a flush, but that was a minor inconvenience.

The bars of the cell door did not reach the ground so that meals could be shoved through without having to unlock the door. Each meal was delivered by an Indian POW accompanied by an armed Pakistani guard. There was no chance of conversation, just the scrape of the thali under the door.

On the second or third day, an Indian jawan came to Dilip's cell as usual and slid the thali through. As soon as the two men had left, Dilip sat down to his meal. When he picked up his roti, he found a piece of paper in the fold. 'Dilip, we are all here. All seven are safe. Welcome to Lyallpur.'

How had his friends discovered he was here, he wondered. Had the Indian jawans who were serving the food passed the word?

From the courtyard Dilip studied the prison's high outer walls topped with electrified barbed wire, and towers manned by armed guards. Lyallpur prison was certainly an impressive place. But no prison is escape-proof, not a hundred per cent. Already he had an idea. He would need rope for a ladder and a hook. He figured he could scale the wall and throw his thin mattress over the wire. But that was weeks away. First he would have to get out of this cage.

# Lyallpur

The last week in August the prison was abuzz with activity. On 31 August the Indian POWs would celebrate Janamashthami, the birth of Lord Krishna. Knowing that Janamashthami was an important Hindu festival, Latif had agreed to a request that the Indian jawans prepare a programme, and all POWs (except the three in solitary confinement) be allowed to attend. But then the requests had kept coming. They needed costumes and a sound system. They needed time to rehearse. All this was good for morale, he supposed, so he said yes to all the requests. In fact, the programme was becoming so impressive that he decided to invite local dignitaries to attend as well. So the set-up became even more elaborate—chairs for the fourteen POW officers, chairs for the dignitaries, and some thought given as to who would sit where. The six hundred jawans, of course, would sit on the ground.

By this time the seven IAF officers had become well acquainted with their seven army counterparts. All the army officers were friendly and helped the newcomers in every possible way. The senior officer, Major Hamir Singh, who had been badly wounded, bore his pain with great stoicism. He was finally repatriated as a medical case a month or so after the IAF officers' arrival. The other six army officers were young men in their twenties.

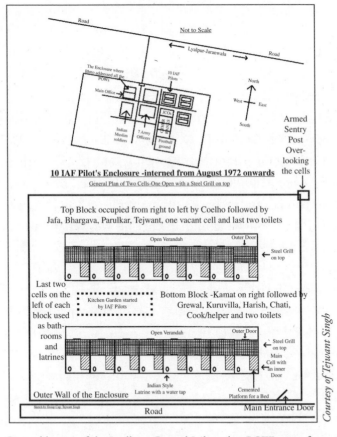

General layout of the Lyallpur Central Jail used as POW camp for Indian Army personnel and Air Force pilots

One of them, Captain Dastur, had been on the same Forward Air Control team as Mulla-Feroze, and blamed the overconfident IAF pilot for his capture. 'I kept telling him we were too far forward, but he said he knew the place like the back of his hand!' It did not sit well with Dastur that Mulla-Feroze had already gone home while he was still cooling his heels in Pakistan.

But the teasing was usually good-natured and they were glad to have one another's company. Every clear evening the officers met to play volleyball. Even Jafa, Singh and Kamat stood their ground and hit the ball when it came within range, though they left the leaps and net shots to Chati and Kuruvilla, who were in better shape. Their most enthusiastic, energetic players were still in the clink, so they had to make do.

Every time the POWs encountered Camp Commandant Latif they would ask him to consider letting their friends out of solitary a few days early. Here we are enjoying good company they would say, but we are thinking of them. And they had the support of the army POWs when they made their requests. But Latif was not about to give in. He would just smile and shake his head, as if to say you are doing your duty and I must do mine, too.

The night of Janamashthami everyone was in a jolly mood from laughing at jokes and the crazy antics of the jawans playing the roles of women. Still, when Latif came by they didn't forget to ask him again. Here we are all together, having fun, they said, if only our friends could be here to enjoy the programme with us. This time Latif's reaction was more promising, 'I'll see what I can do,' he said.

The next day he released all three men from solitary

confinement. His told each of them, 'Because your behaviour has been exemplary, I have decided to release you early.' But their friends told them the story from another angle. We asked him again and again, they said. And the night of Janamashthami, Latif had something at stake as well. He had invited VIPs from Lyallpur to attend. He had six hundred POWs as well as camp staff enjoying the show. He didn't want to refuse us that night. We could have stopped the show if we'd chosen to.

One way or another, depending on who is telling the story, the three escapees were released on 1 September 1972, and joined their comrades in the IAF compound. When the three arrived there were hugs and handshakes all around. Then it was catch-up time, with stories to tell about getting caught by the tehsildar, and political agent Burki and Usman Hamid coming to the rescue; about Dilip's attempt to escape the first night in Peshawar; about the phone call to the camp and the hulchul that followed; about Wahid's anger and Rizvi's hurt feelings. How different Latif was from Wahid-ud-din, they all agreed. No one could ruffle Latif. He was an experienced manager of men. If there was dirty work to be done, he would leave that to others.

But for prisoners at Lyallpur life was, for the most part, a frictionless affair. The high-security prison, which is still in use, was built in the 1960s during the military rule of President Ayub Khan. It was used, at this point, to house criminals and political dissidents, as well as the six hundred prisoners of war. Designed to hold two thousand prisoners, it was far from full. The ten IAF POWs had their own compound, with a cook and two assistants from the Indian Army. They were housed in two rows of cells. Since there were twenty cells and only ten prisoners, the cook and his assistants also slept in the compound, and one cell was allotted for cooking. In each row of cells one of the end cells became the toilet and the other, the bathroom. Though there were toilets in each room, the prisoners preferred this arrangement.

During the day the individual cells were unlocked and the prisoners circulated within the compound freely. The only guard in sight stood on a platform at one corner of the eight-foot wall that bordered their compound. To summon a guard or the havaldar who attended them, they used to take a stick from the cook's stack and whack the metal gate several times.

At first the army POWs had been lodged in civilian prisons or in hospitals along the border. By February they had all been brought to Lyallpur. Conditions at Lyallpur were miserable at first but gradually improved. The army POWs believed that the improvements had happened largely because of simultaneous reciprocity—once the authorities in Pakistan knew their own prisoners were being well taken care of, they were willing to reciprocate. But they had had to push for changes, too. During their early days at Lyallpur the food was poor and there was no opportunity for the officers to meet the jawans and nothing to do all day.

By August when the airmen arrived, all the POWs assembled each Sunday for a religious service. One Sunday the service was Sikh, the next, Hindu and the following, Christian, but everyone attended, except the Muslims (though they did take in programmmes on certain occasions, such as Janamashthami). The privilege of meeting all together, whether on Sunday for prayers or at other times to play football or attend an evening programme, had taken a while to establish. The Pakistani authorities had assumed that the jawans in each religious group would be content to live, eat and socialize separately, and were surprised to find they were not. The men wanted occasions to come together and their officers, who had never been segregated into religious groups, supported them. Still, the jawans did continue to live in separate compounds based on their religion, and sleep side by side on the floor in large barracks.

In some ways Lyallpur was a stricter place than the Pindi camp. There was no TV, no listening to the BBC or All India Radio, no books. They could not send a lascar out for sweets or chapli kababs or a bottle of booze. There were no lascars at Lyallpur. All the staff were military. In any case, they had no cash in hand to bribe an attendant. At the Lyallpur prison canteen all purchases were deducted from each officer's monthly allowance.

The strange thing is, despite the loss of TV in the evenings, and books, and newscasts, the IAF prisoners remember being happier at Lyallpur than they were in Pindi. For one thing, they weren't locked in their cells, except at night. In Pindi, every time they wanted to move from one space to another, from their own cell to Cell 5, or to the toilet, they had to wait for a guard to unlock and lock a door, but at Lyallpur they could move freely around their own compound. And their meals, cooked on site by their countrymen, were much more appetizing. Also, it was good to see some fresh faces. Almost every day they met the seven Indian army officers for tea, or a meal, or a game of chess or bridge or volleyball, usually in the army officers' compound, which was about a hundred metres from their own. Occasionally they played football with the jawans, and on Sundays there was always the gathering of all six hundred POWs for a religious service of one kind or another.

The havaldar who attended their needs was an obliging fellow. They could ask him to fetch soap or shaving cream from the canteen or they could ask him to take them to the canteen themselves. It was always a welcome break. The canteen was well stocked, and if you didn't see what you needed, you could ask and the item would be ordered. Tejwant Singh was able to buy oil paints and cloth that he transformed into canvas for his paintings.

But despite all these distractions, Dilip continued to plan an escape. After all, something that had been tried once, and had almost succeeded, was surely worth another go. And Tejwant Singh developed a plan of his own. When they look back now, both men are amazed and somewhat embarrassed by the naivety of their plans, but at the time those were the ideas that nourished hope for freedom and fed their ingenuity.

This time neither man thought of tunnelling out. There was no ignoring the impressive walls of Lyallpur prison, or the guards posted in the towers. It was a matter of finding a way over those high walls and the tangle of electrified wire on top. Dilip elaborated on his original idea of scaling the high wall (after scaling the wall of the inner compound) and throwing a mattress over the wire. He might need two mattresses, he concluded, and he would definitely need a diversion of some sort. He finally settled on a sandstorm. When the rains ended in September and the winds began to blow and blow, sandstorms were not uncommon. If it were a roaring storm, visibility would be vastly reduced and he believed he could scale the walls without being caught. It would, of course, be a solo effort this time.

Singh's scheme also depended on the winds. He hoped to float over the walls with the aid of a hot air balloon. He would buy sheeting from the canteen and treat it with chemicals as he had the canvases for his paintings. He would use one of the kerosene burners from the kitchen for the flame. He started by devising a miniature model using sticks and cloth and tried it in the space between the two blocks of cells, away from the eyes of the guard on the corner platform. But no matter how he constructed the thing, it was never light enough to travel far, and he eventually gave up trying.

A more successful scheme was brewing a batch of rum. Since there was no Aurangzeb to send out to the market (and no cash in hand to pay him, in any case), the drinking men put their heads together and decided to make their own. It involved buying jaggery from the canteen and mixing it with water in a water pot—the same kind of clay pot found in the corner of every kitchen in India and Pakistan. They would have liked to add some orange peels and a bit of barley, but that was impossible, so they settle for straight jaggery and water.

The function of a water pot is to stay cool and uncontaminated (thus its narrow neck) but in this case they needed warmth. In fact both Singh and Grewal knew that a Punjabi farmer would bury his pot in a layer of manure, but they had none of that either, so they settled on burying the pot of brew in the garden between the two cell blocks, where they already had some carrots and radishes growing. There it would get the sun for at least part of the day. After a week or so, they put an ear to the ground and listened for the burble of fermentation. All this happened out

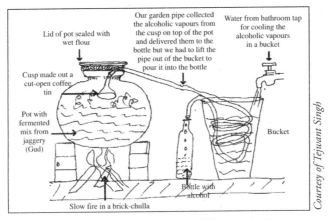

Lid of pot sealed with wet flour

Our garden pipe collected the alcoholic vapours from the cusp on top of the pot and delivered them to the bottle but we had to lift the pipe out of the bucket to pour it into the bottle

Water from bathroom tap for cooling the alcoholic vapours in a bucket

Cusp made out a cut-open coffee tin

Pot with fermented mix from jaggery (Gud)

Bucket

Bottle with alcohol

Slow fire in a brick-chulla

*Courtesy of Tejwant Singh*

Still assembled out of nothing in POW Camp Lyallpur,
November 1972

of view of the guard who sat on his platform at one corner of the compound.

It was a happy day when the burble was detected. In turn each man put an ear to the ground, the drinking men and teetotallers alike, all in on the game. Then it was the turn of Kamat and Singh to set up a still, using sections of garden hose, several tin cans reshaped, and a burner from the kitchen. The distilling took place on a Sunday morning when the others were attending the weekly service. The result was two bottles of brew, but it wasn't the best brew, they discovered that evening. They had been too eager. They should have waited a little longer. Still, everyone had a sample, and nothing was left over.

And so the time passed. By the end of September the rains had stopped and the nights had cooled enough for a decent sleep. By the end of October they needed blankets at night. In November, with temperatures dipping to ten degrees they were already wearing their POW sweaters to bed. They dreaded the winter to come. It would be their second winter in captivity. Three months of being chilled to the bone. Singh bought some material from the canteen and sewed himself a housecoat.

On 8 November, after forty days of fasting during daylight hours, the Muslim POWs celebrated Eid with a special gathering. Coelho, who was senior officer among all the prisoners, remembers persuading everyone to attend.

'It was an opportunity to show the solidarity of being Indian,' he says. He was particularly concerned that some of the forty-two Muslim POWs might defect and choose not to be repatriated. All the POWs, both officers and jawans, did attend the Eid celebration. During the prayers they had to watch their Muslim colleagues carefully so that they could follow along.

'At Eid everyone hugs each other three times,' Coelho remembers. 'By the time we had finished everyone was weeping.'

In November each airman also received a large box sent by the IAF through the International Red Cross. Each box was full of packages of biscuits and tins of food. They realized that their complaints about the poor food in Rawalpindi had been heard—rather late—but heard nevertheless, and now they had not only the better meals in Lyallpur but this bounty to share with their comrades from the army.

A week or so after receiving their parcels, when they crossed over to the army officers' compound for volleyball, the airmen noticed a great clean-up in progress. The larger compound had been scrupulously swept and the paths marked out with limestone powder. An inspection coming up, they guessed, or an important visitor, which was about the same thing. Then, the next day they were told to look sharp for an assembly. The day was Friday, 24 November.

That morning all the IAF prisoners except Bhargava, whose back was troubling him, were taken to a compound near the main gate. All six hundred jawans were already sitting on durries in front of a stage set with a podium and microphone. Flags were flying. Journalists and photographers were gathering near the stage. 'Bhutto is on his way,' their army colleagues predicted. Were they guessing or had they been informed by their havaldar of what was afoot? Soon they heard the sound of helicopters, then the approach of jeeps. A few minutes later President Zulfikar Ali Bhutto stepped out of a jeep and mounted the stage. He needed no introduction.

By this time the POWs expected a momentous announcement. Had the three countries finally agreed to an exchange of prisoners? Was it possible they wouldn't spend another winter in Pakistan after all? But that was not what Bhutto said. They had all been guests in his country far too long, he said, and he had decided, unilaterally, to release them. What India did was up to that country. He had made his decision and it would stand.

He said all this with great flourishes. He would stop and look directly at them with his broad face, or toss his head back. It was an impressive performance. With his thick fringe of grey hair, he was like a lion surveying his territory. At the end of it the POWs applauded politely. Bhutto walked off the stage and left immediately without mingling. He was a popular man still, but not as popular at Lyallpur prison as he was on the outside.

The airmen walked back to their compound eager to tell Bhargava the news. They were going home, and though Bhutto had not said exactly when, they knew a promise is a promise, especially when it is made in public before the TV cameras.

The Indian government was caught by surprise by Bhutto's announcement, but the following Monday Swaran Singh, Minister of Foreign Affairs, announced that India would reciprocate by releasing the 540 Pakistani POWs captured on the western front. Meanwhile, in Lyallpur, the IAF prisoners dug into their food boxes with gusto. They might have only a few days left and they didn't plan to leave anything behind.

# Home

On 30 November, six days after Bhutto's announcement, the IAF officers at Lyallpur were given new uniforms. That evening, 617 prisoners of war (including 17 civilians) were taken in buses to the railway station where they boarded a night train to Lahore. Travelling at night meant less chance of civilian interference. Hostility to India was still widely felt in Pakistan and the authorities didn't want to take any chances. On both the buses and the trains the prisoners travelled without the usual blindfolds and handcuffs, but they were not ready to celebrate yet. Many a slip 'twixt cup and lip, they were thinking, still not quite sure the whole thing would come off.

Early in the next morning the IAF officers and their army counterparts detrained somewhere east of Lahore and were taken to an army mess. They were each given a room in the barracks. It was a clean room, the cleanest room each man had seen in a year and a great contrast to the musty cells they had inhabited. There was even a batman to fetch hot water for a bath and shave. After they had bathed they all had breakfast together, a real breakfast of porridge and eggs and toast with jam. Then they boarded a bus for Wagah.

The village of Wagah, on the Grand Trunk Highway, is the only border crossing between Pakistan and India. The western part of the town is in Pakistan, the eastern part, in India. At the border is a grand arch, with soldiers standing guard on each side. The exchange was to begin at the Wagah border crossing at 10 a.m. In fact, the exchange didn't start until 11.05 a.m. with the 540 Pakistani prisoners going first. And though that part was finished shortly after noon, there was a delay until 2.30 p.m. before the Indian POWs started across.

In the meantime, the IAF prisoners waited their turn to walk through the Wagah arch into India. And sure enough there was a last-minute glitch. When they were within sight of the arch, a PAF Group Captain stopped them.

'India has not sent our airmen,' he told them, 'so we can't let you go.'

They argued that Bhutto had made a promise, a unilateral gesture. He had said he would send them all home no matter what India did. But the Group Captain did not give in. He ordered them to stay where they were and disappeared. They waited anxiously until the matter was finally sorted. (They learned later that the two Pakistani airmen in India were returned the following day.)

Finally they were given the go-ahead to start walking again. Even Bhargava walked across the border though his back was killing him. He didn't want to cross on a stretcher and have his wife see him that way. As usual the POWs were living in an information vacuum, the last ones to know that their families would be waiting for them in Delhi. Only Grewal's family had come to Wagah. As soon as he crossed the border he was greeted by his father, who lived in Amritsar, and his eldest brother who had flown in from America, as well as a cousin.

It was all quite bewildering. P.C. Tandon, a journalist for the *Times of India* reported 'the Pakistani prisoners were grim-faced, a bit lost, somewhat dazed' and 'the returning Indians, too, looked dumb-founded . . . but all of them recovered their composure and cheer within seconds of realizing they really were back home and welcome.'

The government of Punjab gave each man a hero's welcome, 'first a warm pat (as they stepped through the monumental Wagah gate), then garlands and hugs, and a 22-kilometre drive to Amritsar through 100 welcome arches, flags, festoons and bunting, throngs of cheering men and women and children, capped by a rousing civic reception at Amritsar.'

After the reception in Amritsar, the ten IAF officers boarded an Avro 748 for Palam airport near Delhi. Their army colleagues were not pleased at such preferential treatment, but airlifting six hundred POWs was not on the agenda so they had to await an evening train. As soon as the ten airmen stepped off the Avro they were greeted warmly by colleagues, friends and family. Then someone thought of a photo so they mounted the aircraft's steps again.

Dilip's parents and sisters had come, as well as a throng of friends. He had been posted at Palam and Hindon, both near Delhi, so had many friends in the area. Bhargava's wife Anu had come with their children. They were only two and three years old and had no memory of their father. For several days Anu had to remind them to call Bhargava Daddy, not Uncle! Kamat's two little daughters, a few years older, clung to their father and didn't want to let go.

Hope Coelho, with her three children, was 'the picture of joy'. 'My name is Hope,' she told a reporter, 'and that's why I'm always so hopeful.' Also on hand to receive Coelho were two cousins. One of them had flown all the way from Canada.

Young Robin Jafa, almost as articulate as his father, told a *Times of India* reporter, 'We were badly shaken when we learned that dad was taken prisoner, but as the letters began coming after the first two months, we settled down to a long wait.'

The youngest airman, Chati, was greeted by the largest contingent of sixteen relatives from Nagpur. Altogether it was a joyous welcome home with smiles and tears of happiness all round.

The next day, the central government held a reception for all the POWs at the Ram Lila grounds in Old Delhi. It was a hot day for December but no refreshments were served and security was so tight that some relatives were not allowed in. On top of that Defense Minister Jagjivan Ram arrived an hour late. In Amritsar they had felt truly welcomed home, but the Delhi reception seemed to be devised 'for the politicians and not for us'.

On Monday, 4 December, the debriefing began at the IAF Station, New Delhi. Officially called a court of inquiry into the absence of ten airmen, the process involved each man writing an individual report and then sitting through questioning by various groups, including Intelligence. To start with, all ten men were sequestered in the same room with paper and pen to write their reports. It was an opportunity to share memories, to get their stories straight, and to make it clear in their reports that none of them had collaborated with the enemy. What they needed to do was emphasize their unity in resistance. They remembered Jafa's verbal sparring with Wahid-ud-din, the conversations with visiting Pakistani airmen and, most of all, the preparations for the escape. What better evidence of resistance could there be than the escape attempt? And each man had cooperated in that, even if some had been more enthusiastic than others.

The court of inquiry took fifteen days. On one of those days, Dilip met with IAF Chief P.C. Lal in his office and personally presented him with what looked like a fountain pen but was, in fact, a compass.

Then, after a sixty-day leave, they were all posted to their new units. In fact they had a choice of postings but none could be in sensitive areas, not for another two years. Dilip chose Secunderabad, where he had been posted just before the war.

Jafa, Bhargava, and Kamat would never fly fighters again. Because of their injuries the IAF would not allow them to risk another ejection. The other men remained fighter pilots. 'Once again,' remembers Grewal, 'life revolved around a single engine jet, from where everything had started . . . '

After his repatriation, Dilip Parulkar's parents lost little time in arranging his marriage. His mother believed that her son had suffered enough and needed some comfort in his life. On his wedding day, five months after repatriation, Dilip was pleased to receive the following telegram from his friend and co-conspirator, Squadron Leader Kamat: 'No escape from this sweet captivity.'

Grewal, still a bachelor, chose Bareilly for his first posting, and used his 24,000 rupees back pay to buy a Fiat 1200.

And each man, in his own way and in his own time, tried to catch up on all that he had missed, though in some ways you can never catch up. There will always be that tune everyone knows but you, or the memory of a child's first steps, or that word she repeated endlessly when she first began to talk. When you have been away from everything familiar for a year, some things are irretrievable.

But in the wider world, little had changed. Mrs Gandhi was still the prime minister of India, her popularity high because of the war they'd helped win. While they twiddled their thumbs in Lyallpur, Richard Nixon, no friend of India, had been re-elected president of the United States by a landslide. They learned that the Munich Olympics, which Grewal and Parulkar had hoped to see, ended in a massacre of Israeli athletes by a Palestinian group called Black September. No, there wasn't much new. Even though the Vietnam War was winding down, the world was still an arbitrary place, and a dangerous one, too.

# Epilogue

When **Aditya Vikram Pethia** returned to India in May 1972, he was diagnosed as having a pulmonary haematoma caused by his severe beating. He gradually recovered and in 1973 he was back to flying fighters. He was awarded the Vir Chakra for gallantry in operations on 5 December 1971, the day his Mystere was shot down. He retired from the IAF as Air Vice-Marshal in 2001. He lives in Bhopal.

**Dilip Parulkar** was awarded the Vayu Sena Medal for landing his crippled aircraft in the 1965 war. In 1983 he was awarded the Vishisht Seva Medal for dedicated and distinguished service. His valour in leading an escape attempt in 1971 was cited. Parulkar retired from the IAF as Group Captain in 1987. He lives in Pune.

**Malvinder Singh Grewal** left the IAF in 1984 to manage his family farm. He was awarded the Vir Chakra for gallantry in operations on 5 December 1971, the day his Sukhoi 7 was shot down. He currently lives at Bharaya Co-operative Farms, Bilaspur, Uttar Pradesh.

**Harish Sinhji** retired from the IAF as Wing Commander in 1993. His vivid description of the escape from the Rawalpindi POW camp was published as an appendix to P.C. Lal's *My Years in the IAF* (1986). Sinhji died in 2004. His children Kaveri and Vikram live in Bangalore.

**Bernard Anthony Coelho** became the chief flying instructor at an IAF flying school and subsequently held a staff appointment (operations). He retired from the IAF as Air Vice-Marshal in 1986. He lives in Noida.

When he returned to India, **Dhirendra Singh Jafa** was unable to fly on account of spinal injuries. He retired from the IAF in 1974. He was awarded the Vayu Sena Medal before the 1971 war for his dedication in ensuring that his squadron was operational on the Sukhoi 7 in the shortest possible time. After the war he was awarded the Vir Chakra for gallantry and leadership in operations on 4–5 December 1971. In 1999 he published a novel, *Three Countries, One People,* based largely on his experiences during the wars of 1965 and 1971 and his year as a POW. He lives in Faizabad, Uttar Pradesh.

**Arun Vithal Kamat** was unable to fly fighters again because of his injuries. He was awarded the Vayu Sena Medal for gallantry in operations on 9 December 1971, the day his Marut went down and he broke both his legs. He remained in the IAF until his untimely death in 1982.

Although unable to fly fighters again because of his injured back, **Jawahar Lal Bhargava** did fly helicopters. He retired from the IAF as Air Commodore in 1995. His writings about his capture and prisoner of war experience are posted on the marutfans website. He currently lives in Gurgaon.

In April, 1973, **Tejwant Singh** managed to land his Mig-21 after its canopy had been shattered in a collision with a vulture. He was awarded the Shaurya Chakra, a peacetime gallantry award, for displaying courage and professionalism of a high order. Although one of his eyes had been seriously hurt in the collision, he recovered and returned once more to flying. He retired from the IAF as Group Captain in 1994. He currently lives in Gurgaon and writes fiction full time.

**Kariyadil Cheriyan Kuruvilla** returned to flying fighters. He was awarded the Vir Chakra for displaying gallantry in operations in the western sector during 4–6 December 1971. He retired from the IAF as Air Commodore in 2001. He currently lives in Bangalore.

**Hufrid N.D. Mulla-Feroze,** the first POW to be repatriated, recovered from his injuries. He retired from the IAF in 1992 and died in 2011.

**Vidyadhar Shankar Chati** returned to flying fighters and then spent many years as a flying instructor in the IAF. He retired from the IAF as Wing Commander in 1990 to take up a career in civil aviation. Altogether he logged over 9000 hours of flying time. He currently lives in Secunderabad.

The 1971 Indo-Pakistan War, though less than two weeks long, produced the highest casualties of all Indo-Pakistani conflicts (approximately 13,000 killed and 14,000 wounded) and the greatest numbers of POWs since World War II. In light of these statistics, the twelve IAF officers held in No. 3 Provost and Security Flight in Rawalpindi were among the lucky ones.

The Pakistani soldiers captured on the eastern front were

held prisoner for almost two years. Finally in September 1973, after the signing of the Delhi Accord, the 93,000 POWs held in India and some 200,000 Bangladeshis stranded in Pakistan were allowed to return home. In 1974, in return for Pakistani recognition and a settling of accounts, Bangladesh permitted 195 men it had identified as war criminals to return to Pakistan without trial.

In October 1974, the Hamoodur Rahman Commission appointed by Bhutto to investigate Pakistan's 1971 surrender made its final report. It found that in Bangladesh some members of the Pakistan Army had been guilty of mass killings of both civilians and Bengali officers, and had used rape as a deliberate act of revenge. However, the commission estimated the number of civilian deaths to be much lower than 2,00,000, the most conservative estimate made by other groups. Still the entire report was so damning that it was classified for years. In 2000, parts of the leaked document were published in both India and Pakistan. In December that year the whole document was finally declassified.

On 9 August 1974, Richard Nixon, who had ignored the killing in East Pakistan in order to facilitate détente with China, resigned as president of the United States before he could be impeached for the Watergate scandal. Sheikh Mujibur Rahman, an early inmate of the prison at Lyallpur, served as prime minister of Bangladesh until he was assassinated in a military coup on 24 January 1975. Zulfikar Ali Bhutto, whose unilateral initiative resulted in the exchange of prisoners captured on the western front, was deposed in a military coup and executed on 4 April 1979. Indira Gandhi was assassinated on 31 October 1984.

The peace established between India and Pakistan by the Simla Agreement has held, so far. Though tensions have mounted on a number of occasions, and battles were fought on the Line of Control at Kargil in 1999, the two countries have not gone to war for the last forty years.

# Timeline
## Bangladesh War of Independence and
## Indo-Pakistan War 1971

| | |
|---|---|
| **December 1970/ January 1971** | In the first general election in Pakistan since 1945, the Awami League of East Pakistan wins a majority of seats in the National Assembly. |
| **1 March 1971** | President Yahya Khan of Pakistan announces that the National Assembly will not meet as scheduled. Mass demonstrations begin in East Pakistan. |
| **25 March 1971** | The Pakistan Army, under orders, begins to round up and execute supporters of the Awami League, students at Dacca university, known intellectuals and many others. The Awami league is banned. Its leader, Sheikh Mujibur Rahman, is arrested. An estimated 2,00,000 will die at the hands of the military. |
| **26 March 1971** | The Awami League declares the independence of Bangladesh. |

# Timeline

| | |
|---|---|
| **April 1971** | India shelters an estimated 4 million refugees from Bangladesh. That number will grow to close to 10 million. |
| **May 1971** | India starts aiding the resistance in East Pakistan (the Mukti Bahini) and prepares for war. |
| **3 December 1971** | Pakistan launches air raids on Indian Air Force bases. India declares war on Pakistan. |
| **7 December 1971** | India recognizes the independence of Bangladesh. |
| **16 December 1971** | All Pakistani troops in Bangladesh surrender. |
| **17 December 1971** | India and Pakistan agree to a ceasefire. India holds approximately 93,000 prisoners of war; Pakistan, less than 1000. |
| **20 December 1971** | Yahya Khan resigns. Zulfikar Ali Bhutto becomes president of Pakistan. |
| **2 July 1972** | The Simla Agreement outlines the plans for withdrawal of troops and normalization of relations between India and Pakistan. It does not include an exchange of POWs. |
| **24 November 1972** | In a unilateral gesture Bhutto announces that he is sending the Indian POWs home. |
| **1 December 1972** | All POWs captured on the western front are exchanged. |
| **28 August 1973** | India and Pakistan sign the Delhi Accord. It allows the release of 93,000 Pakistani POWs held in India and over 2,00,000 Bangladeshis stranded in Pakistan. |

# Bibliography

**Published Sources**

Ahamed, Syeed, The Curious Case of 195 War Criminals, *The Forum*, May 2010 (http://www.thedailystar.net/forum/2010/may/curious.htm)

*A Handbook for Travellers in India, Burma and Ceylon*, 13th edition (John Murray 1929)

Bass, Gary J., *The Blood Telegram, Nixon, Kissinger, and a Forgotten Genocide* (Alfred A. Knopf 2013)

Chowdhary, Lt. Col. S.S., *I Was a Prisoner of War in Pakistan* (Lancer International 1985)

Jafa, D.S., *Three Countries One People* (Minerva Press 1999)

Jagan Mohan, P.V.S. and Chopra, Samir, *The Indian–Pakistan War of 1965* (Manohar 2005)

Khan, Arshad Sami, *Three Presidents and an Aid* (Pentagon Press 2008)

Lal, P.C., *My Years with the I.A.F* (Lancer, 2nd edition, 2008)

# Bibliography

Quasim, Syed Shah Abul, 'Excerpts: Life in Camp 29,' *Life Story of an Ex-Soldier,* self-published (http://archives.dawn.com/weekly/booksarchive/030427/books3.htm

Sinhji, Harish, 'The Escape Story,' from P.C. Lal, *My Years with the I.A.F.* pp. 346–69

Talbot, Ian, *Pakistan, a New History* (Amaryllis 2012)

*Times of India* 1972

**Unpublished Sources**

Athale, Anil, *Memories of a Prisoner of War,* 6 December 2010, http://uswww.rediff.com

Bhargava, Jawahar Lal, *How I Got Captured* and *POW Saga Parts I–VIII,* http:marutfans,wordpress.com

Grewal, M.S., *Gary 1971*

Parulkar, Dilip, letters to Inder Khanna: 14 April 1963, 28 April and 10 October 1964, undated (from the UK), 10 October 1965, 9 January 1972, 7 March 1972

Singh H.K., *Story of a Hunter Pilot- 71 War*

Singh, Tejwant, *Visit to Historical Gurdwara Punja Sahib at Hasan Abdal, In the Aftermath of the Escape, Other Experiences in the POW Camp Rawalpindi, Other Experiences in the POW camp Lyallpur*

**Interviews**

Bhargava, Jawahar Lal
Coelho, Bernard Anthony
Grewal, Malvinder Singh

Jafa, Dhirendra Singh
Kuruvilla, Kariyadil Cheriyan
Parulkar, Dilip
Pethia, Aditya Vikram
Singh, Tejwant
Sinjhi, Kaveri

# Acknowledgements

My first thanks must be to my husband, Air Commodore Manbir Singh Vr.C,VM (retired) who suggested that I write this story and provided his support and technical knowledge all along the way.

Without Dilip Parulkar, there would be no story. I thank him for his good humour in answering many questions, digging up material, suggesting books to read, and introducing me to other POWs.

I have never met Harish Sinhji, who died in 2004, but I have him to thank for some of the most vivid details of the night of the escape and the capture the next morning. He was the first of the POWs to write about his experience. Fortunately his account was published as an appendix to the memoir of Air Chief P.C. Lal in 1986.

Soon after I began this project I asked Grewal, Dilip's partner, to record his memories of capture and escape. The other POWs called him Gary, so he labelled his account *Gary 1971*. That document has been valuable in itself and has been the starting point for many questions.

Eventually I was able to get in touch with Pethia, Jafa, Kuruvilla, Coelho, Bhargava, Tejwant Singh, and Kaveri and Vikram Sinhji. Without exception, each person has cooperated in this project by answering questions and, in some cases, offering new insights.

I thank Jawahar Lal Bhargava and Tejwant Singh for being particularly generous in sharing materials with me. Both men are writers themselves and could have regarded me as an intruder on their territory, but the reaction of each man was the opposite. Bhargava provided me with several of his writings on the web that I had missed and answered many, many questions. Tejwant Singh shared his memories and introduced me to Coelho, Kuruvilla, Pethia and Kaveri Sinhji. As well as suggesting books for me to read, he provided most of the photos and maps for this book.

Thanks also to my agent Kanishka Gupta (The Writer's Side) for recognizing the merits of this book, and to Meru Gokhale and Archana Shankar of Random House India for facilitating its production.